HackneyandJones.com

Writers and Publishers

Hackney and Jones

HACKNEY & JONES

Just some of the books we have written...

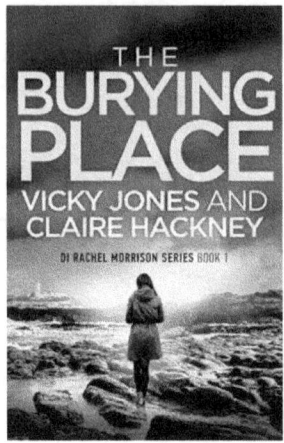
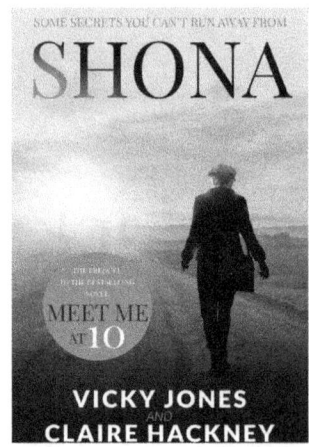
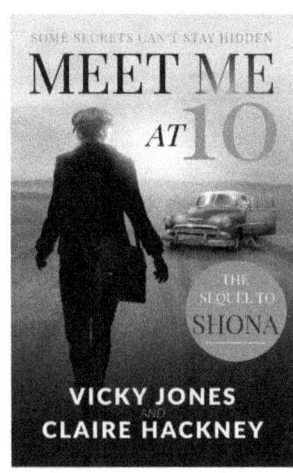

GRAB YOUR FREE BOOK HERE:

SIMPLY SCAN THE QR CODE BELOW

How To Write A Novel From Scratch

Writing a book has never been so easy –
Just fill in the blanks!

Find our products/resources at:

HackneyandJones.com

What EXACTLY is this book about?

It is an easy-to-use workbook that guides you from a blank page with NO ideas to a compelling first draft ready for the editor. It is a proven guide (that we use) to ensure your book includes everything to make it compelling to read.

Who is it for?

Beginners to seasoned pros who want a no-fuss way to get their first draft done.

How do I use it?

Follow the steps and you'll build your book as you go to where it will appear almost effortlessly before your eyes!

This workbook is perfectly accompanied by 'The Ultimate Guide To Novel Writing For Beginners'

Order NOW:

THE FICTION SQUARE

USE THE FICTION SQUARES IN THE NEXT FEW PAGES TO COME UP WITH ENDLESS IDEAS.

FOR EXAMPLE:

SAY IF YOU PICK THE FOLLOWING:

SOLDIER, LETTER, BEACH, LOVE, RUNNING OUT OF TIME

SO MY MAIN CHARACTER IS A SOLDIER WHO MAYBE GETS HANDED A LETTER FROM A DYING SOLDIER WHO IS ON THE BEACH IN WORLD WAR 2.

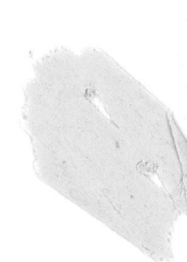

HE'S RUNNING OUT OF TIME AND NEEDS TO DELIVER THIS LOVE LETTER TO SOMEBODY BEFORE THEY ARE DUE TO GET MARRIED TO SOMEBODY ELSE.

THIS WAS JUST THE FIRST IDEA.

NOW OVER TO YOU...

THE FICTION SQUARE

NEED TO COME UP WITH IDEAS?

USE THIS FICTION SQUARE TO CREATE ENDLESS IDEAS! PICK ONE THING FROM EACH COLUMN AND USE THESE AS YOUR INSPIRATION.

CHARACTER OCCUPATION	OBJECT	SETTING/ LOCATION	MOTIVATION	OBSTACLE
SOLDIER	KEY	BEACH	JUSTICE	RUNNING OUT OF TIME
PRINCESS	CAR	CHURCH	GREED	HEALTH
TEACHER	LETTER	SCHOOL	LOVE	SECRET GETS EXPOSED
DOCTOR	A CLOCK	ANOTHER PLANET	SUCCESS	TRAPPED

THE FICTION SQUARE

NOW IT'S YOUR TURN!

Use this blank fiction square to create endless ideas!

CHARACTER OCCUPATION	OBJECT	SETTING/ LOCATION	MOTIVATION	OBSTACLE

THE FICTION SQUARE

NOW IT'S YOUR TURN!

USE THIS BLANK FICTION SQUARE TO CREATE ENDLESS IDEAS!

CHARACTER OCCUPATION	OBJECT	SETTING/ LOCATION	MOTIVATION	OBSTACLE

THE FICTION SQUARE

NOW IT'S YOUR TURN!

USE THIS BLANK FICTION SQUARE TO CREATE ENDLESS IDEAS!

CHARACTER OCCUPATION	OBJECT	SETTING/ LOCATION	MOTIVATION	OBSTACLE

THE FICTION SQUARE

NOW IT'S YOUR TURN!

USE THIS BLANK FICTION SQUARE TO CREATE ENDLESS IDEAS!

CHARACTER OCCUPATION	OBJECT	SETTING/ LOCATION	MOTIVATION	OBSTACLE

THE FICTION SQUARE

NOW IT'S YOUR TURN!

WRITE DOWN YOUR BEST 3-5 IDEAS HERE:

YOUR TITLE

WHAT TO DO

THINK OF WHAT YOUR BOOK IS ABOUT.

NOW LOOK UP AS MANY WORDS AS YOU CAN THAT ARE ASSOCIATED WITH THOSE WORDS.

WHAT IS THE THEME?

THINK OF THE TITLES THAT ARE ALREADY IN YOUR GENRE.

WHICH WORDS COULD MAKE IT INTRIGUING?

WHAT ARE THE QUESTIONS THAT YOUR TITLE IS ASKING?

YOUR TITLE

SUM UP THE BOOK:

NOW, LOOK AT THE 'PATTERNS' OF OTHER TITLES IN YOUR GENRE. (LOOK ON AMAZON) IS THERE A CERTAIN OBJECT, THEME, NAME OR PLACE THAT WOULD MAKE A COMPELLING TITLE?

YOUR TITLE

WHAT QUESTIONS ARE RAISED IN THE READER THAT COULD BE ANSWERED BY THEM READING THE BOOK?

NOW, CHOOSE YOUR MOST COMPELLING TITLE OPTION. IT SHOULD MAKE SENSE TO THE READER.

YOUR TITLE

TITLE OPTION #1

WHAT QUESTIONS DOES THIS TITLE ASK?

# YOUR TITLE

TITLE OPTION #2

WHAT QUESTIONS DOES THIS TITLE ASK?

YOUR TITLE

TITLE OPTION #3

WHAT QUESTIONS DOES THIS TITLE ASK?

GENRE BUNDLE: CRIME

GENRE BUNDLE

THIS IS THE SECRET WEAPON!

WE RESEARCHED THE BESTSELLERS ON AMAZON IN THE CRIME/MYSTERY/HORROR/PSYCHOLOGICAL GENRE IN ORDER TO PRODUCE THE FOLLOWING. YOU CAN USE THIS OR DO THE RESEARCH YOURSELF FOR ANOTHER GENRE.

- POWER WORDS USED IN THE DESCRIPTIONS ON AMAZON.
- MOST USED CHARACTER NAMES IN THAT GENRE.
- FRONT COVER EXAMPLES IN THAT GENRE.
- JOB ROLES MOST USED IN THAT GENRE.
- MOST COMMON EVENTS USED IN THAT GENRE.
- MOST COMMON LOCATIONS USED IN THAT GENRE.
- MOST COMMON WORDS USED IN TITLES IN THAT GENRE.
- DO'S AND DON'T'S OF THAT GENRE (FROM REVIEWS).

AND MUCH MORE!

<u>HOW DO I USE THIS?</u>
THIS IS THE TEMPLATE/FORMULA YOU CAN USE TO ENSURE THAT YOU MODEL WHAT THE BESTSELLERS ARE DOING AND WHAT YOUR READERS ARE EXPECTING.

GENRE BUNDLE: CRIME

NOTE: THIS BUNDLE CAN ALSO INCLUDE THRILLER, MYSTERY, PSYCHOLOGICAL AND HORROR FICTION.

WORDS MOST FREQUENTLY USED IN BLURBS:

DETECTIVE, CASE, DISCOVER, GIRL, HOME, MURDER, BODY, DEAD, DARK, WOMAN, HOUSE, YOUNG, YEARS, BEHIND, DISAPPEARED, FRIEND, FEAR, FOUND, HELP, HAPPENED, HUSBAND, WIFE, INVESTIGATION, MISSING, KILLER, SECRETS, POLICE, PERFECT, VICTIM, WATCHING, TRUTH, REVEALS, PAST, MAN, KNOWS, FAMILY, CITY, KEEP, KILL, EVIDENCE, VANISHED.

HOW CAN I USE THIS? WHAT IMAGES OR THOUGHTS DOES IT EVOKE? IF YOU JOINED UP SOME WORDS (BRAINSTORM) CAN YOU COME UP WITH AN IDEA?

THE WORDS I PICKED TO USE: GIRL, FRIEND, POLICE, PERFECT, WATCHING, FAMILY, MURDER.

MY EXAMPLE:

A YOUNG GIRL IS REPORTED MISSING BY HER BEST FRIEND.

THE POLICE INVESTIGATE WHAT LOOKS TO NOW BE A MURDER.

THE BEST FRIEND COMES FROM A PERFECT FAMILY AND WHEN DCI THOMAS STARTS WATCHING THE FAMILY MORE CLOSELY, NOT EVERYTHING IS AS IT SEEMS...

GENRE BUNDLE: CRIME

NOTE: THIS BUNDLE CAN ALSO INCLUDE THRILLER, MYSTERY, PSYCHOLOGICAL AND HORROR FICTION.

CHARACTER NAMES AND ROLES:

HUSBAND, WIFE, YOUNG GIRL. LUCY, ELIZA, KERRY, EX-HUSBAND. RENEE, CATHERINE, GEORGE, ALISON, RUTH, ADAM, EDEN, LILY, ALICE, ALICIA, JULES, WILL, IN-LAWS, GEMMA, ELLIOT, CHLOE, PARENTS, A STRANGER, SUZI, NORA, ELLE, KIDNAPPER, YOUNG GIRLS, MOLLY, ELLA, ANNA, SARAH, PARENTS, TWINS, SISTERS, HOMELESS MAN/WOMAN, NEIGHBOURS, DAUGHTER, TAMSYN, EDIE, BEN, SOPHIE, EMMA, NINA, MAGGIE, ALISON, A COLLEAGUE, A CLIENT, ROY, LAURA, MEG, AN ELDERLY WOMAN, JIMMY, FEUDING FAMILY MEMBERS, A FISHERMAN, TOM, TAMARA, FREYA, A DOCTOR, A TENANT, SKYE, DAVID, AMY, LILLIAN, ZOE, RUTH, ROSIE, NICK, A BETRAYED WIFE/HUSBAND, SAMANTHA, FRANCES, A PATIENT, CONNIE, LEWIS, STELLA, AN ALCOHOLIC, A CORONER, THE COMMUNITY, TRUDY, CLAIRE, BILLIE, KATE, RESEARCH ASSISTANT, POLICE DETECTIVE, SARA, ERICA, FAITH, MIA, JANIE, A CHILD, EMERGENCY SERVICES, CONSTRUCTION WORKERS, JACK, GANG LEADERS.

HOW CAN I USE THIS? LOTS OF PEOPLE HAVE TOLD ME THEY STRUGGLE TO COME UP WITH CHARACTER NAMES SUITABLE FOR THAT GENRE. THE NAMES AND JOB ROLES ARE THOSE THAT APPEAR WITHIN THE TOP 50 IN THE GENRE.

WHAT DO WE HAVE NOW?

A YOUNG GIRL IS REPORTED MISSING BY HER BEST FRIEND.

THE POLICE INVESTIGATE WHAT LOOKS TO NOW BE A MURDER.

THE BEST FRIEND COMES FROM A PERFECT FAMILY AND WHEN DCI THOMAS STARTS WATCHING THE FAMILY MORE CLOSELY, NOT EVERYTHING IS AS IT SEEMS...

MY CHARACTERS ARE CALLED:
SOPHIE: THE YOUNG GIRL MISSING, 12 YEARS OLD.
ALICE: THE BEST FRIEND, 13 YEARS OLD.
MEG: THE MOTHER OF THE BEST FRIEND, HAS A DRINK PROBLEM.
BEN: THE FATHER OF THE BEST FRIEND IS A CONSTRUCTION WORKER.
DCI TOM NICHOLS: DETECTIVE LOOKING INTO IT.

GENRE BUNDLE: CRIME

NOTE: THIS BUNDLE CAN ALSO INCLUDE THRILLER, MYSTERY, PSYCHOLOGICAL AND HORROR FICTION.

EVENTS:
DINNER PARTY, WEDDING, FUNERAL, PARTY, COURT TRIAL, CELEBRATION.

HOW CAN I USE THIS? MANY BOOKS HAVE A CENTRAL LOCATION OR SOMETHING THAT IS BUILDING UP TOWARDS, OR ITS INCIDENT IS A RESULT OF AN EVENT, I.E. SOMEBODY WAS MURDERED AT A WEDDING RECEPTION OR SOMEBODY IS PLANNING TO MURDER SOMEBODY AT THE WEDDING RECEPTION.

WHAT DO WE HAVE NOW?

A YOUNG GIRL IS REPORTED MISSING BY HER BEST FRIEND.

THE POLICE INVESTIGATE WHAT LOOKS TO NOW BE A MURDER.

THE BEST FRIEND COMES FROM A PERFECT FAMILY AND WHEN DCI THOMAS STARTS WATCHING THE FAMILY MORE CLOSELY, NOT EVERYTHING IS AS IT SEEMS...

MY CHARACTERS ARE CALLED:
SOPHIE: THE YOUNG GIRL MISSING, 12 YEARS OLD.
ALICE: THE BEST FRIEND, 13 YEARS OLD.
MEG: THE MOTHER OF THE BEST FRIEND, HAS A DRINK PROBLEM.
BEN: THE FATHER OF THE BEST FRIEND IS A CONSTRUCTION WORKER.
DCI TOM NICHOLS: DETECTIVE LOOKING INTO IT.

EVENT:
IT IS AT THE YOUNG GIRL'S FUNERAL THAT DCI TOM NICHOLS NOTICES THAT THE MOTHER OF THE BEST FRIEND IS ACTING SUSPICIOUSLY.

GENRE BUNDLE: CRIME

NOTE: THIS BUNDLE CAN ALSO INCLUDE THRILLER, MYSTERY, PSYCHOLOGICAL AND HORROR FICTION.

LOCATIONS:
CITY, IN THE HOME, AT A HOUSE, TOWN, WOODS, RURAL COMMUNITY, MOUNTAINS, HILLS, THE BEACH, ON THE COAST, ISOLATED COTTAGE, TRAIN, THE STREETS, HOSPITAL, ATTIC, AN APARTMENT, VILLAGE, PRISON, AN ASYLUM, BUNKERS, SCHOOL, ALONG A CANAL, IN THE OFFICE.

HOW CAN I USE THIS? MANY BOOKS HAVE A CENTRAL LOCATION OR SOMETHING THAT IS BUILDING UP TOWARDS, OR ITS INCIDENT IS A RESULT OF AN EVENT, I.E. SOMEBODY WAS MURDERED AT A WEDDING RECEPTION OR SOMEBODY IS PLANNING TO MURDER SOMEBODY AT THE WEDDING RECEPTION.

WHAT DO WE HAVE NOW?

A YOUNG GIRL IS REPORTED MISSING BY HER BEST FRIEND.
THE POLICE INVESTIGATE WHAT LOOKS TO NOW BE A MURDER.
THE BEST FRIEND COMES FROM A PERFECT FAMILY AND WHEN DCI THOMAS STARTS WATCHING THE FAMILY MORE CLOSELY, NOT EVERYTHING IS AS IT SEEMS...

MY CHARACTERS ARE CALLED:
SOPHIE: THE YOUNG GIRL MISSING, 12 YEARS OLD.
ALICE: THE BEST FRIEND, 13 YEARS OLD.
MEG: THE MOTHER OF THE BEST FRIEND, HAS A DRINK PROBLEM.
BEN: THE FATHER OF THE BEST FRIEND IS A CONSTRUCTION WORKER.
DCI TOM NICHOLS: DETECTIVE LOOKING INTO IT.

EVENT:
IT IS AT THE YOUNG GIRL'S FUNERAL THAT DCI TOM NICHOLS NOTICES THAT THE MOTHER OF THE BEST FRIEND IS ACTING SUSPICIOUSLY.

LOCATIONS:

THE FAMILY LIVE IN AN ISOLATED COTTAGE ON THE OUTSKIRTS OF A TOWN.

GENRE BUNDLE: CRIME

NOTE: THIS BUNDLE CAN ALSO INCLUDE THRILLER, MYSTERY, PSYCHOLOGICAL AND HORROR FICTION.

TITLES:
HER FINAL WORDS, TRUST NO ONE, THE LATE SHOW, A PLACE OF EXECUTION, THE HOUSE GUEST, I FOUND YOU, THE SILENT PATIENT, THE GUEST LIST, HERE TO STAY, THE OTHER WIFE, PAPER GIRLS, THE PERFECT LIFE, I AM WATCHING YOU, THE GIRL WHO LIVED TWICE, THE COUPLE NEXT DOOR, THE CLIFF HOUSE, THE FRIEND, WHAT LIES BETWEEN US, THE CHALK MAN, DOWN AMONG THE DEAD, BLOOD ORANGE, FIND THEM DEAD, RED BONES, KILL OUR SINS, THE APARTMENT, BURY YOUR PAST, NO ONE HOME, LEFT FOR DEAD, THICKER THAN BLOOD, COFFIN ROAD, THE DEVIL'S CLIFF KILLINGS, THE MISSING, THE BONE JAR, THE GIRL I USED TO BE, A FATAL OBSESSION, SEE THEM RUN, THREE LITTLE PIGS, THE LIAR'S GIRL, NINE ELMS, THE SILENT WIFE, ALL THE RAGE, THREE PERFECT LIARS, LOCKDOWN, BLUE MOON.

WHAT DO WE HAVE NOW?
TITLE (USING THE FORMULA OF 3 WORDS EVOKING QUESTIONS): THE BEST FRIEND; THE TALKING WALLS; THE SILENT VOICE; THE COTTAGE LIE; SECRETS WITHIN WALLS.

A YOUNG GIRL IS REPORTED MISSING BY HER BEST FRIEND.
THE POLICE INVESTIGATE WHAT LOOKS TO NOW BE A MURDER.
THE BEST FRIEND COMES FROM A PERFECT FAMILY AND WHEN DCI THOMAS STARTS WATCHING THE FAMILY MORE CLOSELY, NOT EVERYTHING IS AS IT SEEMS...

MY CHARACTERS ARE CALLED:
SOPHIE: THE YOUNG GIRL GONE MISSING, 12 YEARS OLD.
ALICE: THE BEST FRIEND, 13 YEARS OLD.
MEG: THE MOTHER OF THE BEST FRIEND HAS A DRINK PROBLEM.
BEN: THE FATHER OF THE BEST FRIEND IS A CONSTRUCTION WORKER.
DCI TOM NICHOLS: DETECTIVE LOOKING INTO IT.

EVENT:
IT IS AT THE YOUNG GIRL'S FUNERAL THAT DCI TOM NICHOLS NOTICES THAT THE MOTHER OF THE BEST FRIEND IS ACTING SUSPICIOUSLY.

LOCATIONS:
THE FAMILY LIVE IN AN ISOLATED COTTAGE ON THE OUTSKIRTS OF A TOWN.

GENRE BUNDLE: CRIME

NOTE: THIS BUNDLE CAN ALSO INCLUDE THRILLER, MYSTERY, PSYCHOLOGICAL AND HORROR FICTION.

POWER WORDS:

SHOCKING, CONFESSES, CONFESSION, DISTURBING, CHILLING, UNSETTLING, OBSESSION, DANGEROUS, HIDING, GRIPPING, RECKLESS, SLITHERS, SINISTER, UNRAVEL, BRUTAL, RIVETING, TERRIFIED, STRANGERS, REVELATIONS, CREEPY, SUSPICIONS, MISTAKE, CHILLING, SECRETS, TWISTY, JEALOUSY, HIDDEN, TRAPPED, MOTIVE, MYSTERIOUS, SCARS, CONSEQUENCES, BETRAYAL, HAUNTED, BROKEN, CLUES, DARK/DARKEST, EVIL, HORRIFYING, JAW-DROPPING, DECEIT, DECEPTIVE, NIGHTMARE, THREAT, MISSING, DISAPPEARED, GUILT, FEAR, WATCHING, STALKING, UNDERWORLD, DEADLY, DEATHLY, SILENCE, SLEEPING, LOSS, TRAGIC, TRUST, UNFORGIVABLE, DANGER, POWERLESS, DISCOVER, ACCIDENT, REMAINS, INVESTIGATION, REVELATIONS, HEART-STOPPING, SENSELESS CRIME, MYSTERY, DISFIGURED, GHOSTS, INTENSE, MISADVENTURE, SACRIFICE, SINS, CONSCIENCE, UNFAMILIAR, CONCEALED, SUSPECT, ENEMIES, MOTIVE, PSYCHOPATH, FORENSICS, MO, SERIAL KILLER, DEPRAVED, BLOOD, DEATH, CASUALTY, CORPSE, REMOTE, ISOLATED, SUICIDE, ABANDONED, PERILOUS, CORRUPTION, VIOLENT, UNRESOLVED, INTIMIDATION, FORGOTTEN, REGRET, PUZZLE, GRISLY, ESCAPE, HIT-AND-RUN, UNCOVER, LINK, SEARCH, REELING, HELL, A COPYCAT, NOTORIOUS, HORRIFIC, ELECTRIFYING, CATASTROPHIC, AFRAID, PREDATOR, LINGERS, SHADOWS, VICTIM, WITNESSES, COLD-CASE, ABDUCTION, ATTACK, ASSAULT, ATTACKER, BONES, DECOMPOSED, CONSPIRACY, VIRUS.

WHAT DO WE HAVE NOW?

TITLE (USING THE FORMULA OF 3 WORDS EVOKING QUESTIONS): THE BEST FRIEND; THE TALKING WALLS; THE SILENT VOICE; THE COTTAGE LIE; SECRETS WITHIN WALLS.

A YOUNG GIRL IS REPORTED MISSING BY HER BEST FRIEND.
THE POLICE INVESTIGATE WHAT LOOKS TO NOW BE A MURDER.
THE BEST FRIEND COMES FROM A PERFECT FAMILY AND WHEN DCI THOMAS STARTS WATCHING THE FAMILY MORE CLOSELY, NOT EVERYTHING IS AS IT SEEMS...

MY CHARACTERS ARE CALLED:

SOPHIE: THE YOUNG GIRL GONE MISSING, 12 YEARS OLD.
ALICE: THE BEST FRIEND, 13 YEARS OLD.
MEG: THE MOTHER OF THE BEST FRIEND HAS A DRINK PROBLEM.
BEN: THE FATHER OF THE BEST FRIEND IS A CONSTRUCTION WORKER.
DCI TOM NICHOLS: DETECTIVE LOOKING INTO IT.

EVENT: IT IS AT THE YOUNG GIRL'S FUNERAL THAT DCI TOM NICHOLS NOTICES THAT THE MOTHER OF THE BEST FRIEND IS ACTING SUSPICIOUSLY.

LOCATIONS: THE FAMILY LIVE IN AN ISOLATED COTTAGE ON THE OUTSKIRTS OF A TOWN.
POWER WORDS: DISTURBING, CHILLING, SECRETS, SILENCE, SLEEPING, MISSING, SUSPECT, MYSTERY, VICTIM.

GENRE BUNDLE: CRIME

NOTE: THIS BUNDLE CAN ALSO INCLUDE THRILLER, MYSTERY, PSYCHOLOGICAL AND HORROR FICTION.

WORD COUNT: 65,000

HOW CAN I USE THIS? THIS TELLS ME ROUGHLY HOW LONG MY BOOK WILL BE ACCORDING TO THE GENRE AND WHAT READERS EXPECT.

WRITING SCHEDULE: 8,125 WORDS PER WEEK - BOOK WRITTEN IN 8 WEEKS

HOW CAN I USE THIS? IF YOU WRITE 4 TIMES A WEEK, WRITE APPROXIMATELY 2,031 WORDS EACH SESSION

NOTES:

GENRE BUNDLE: CRIME

NOTE: THIS BUNDLE CAN ALSO INCLUDE THRILLER, MYSTERY, PSYCHOLOGICAL AND HORROR FICTION.

DO'S AND DON'T'S FOR THIS GENRE

HOW CAN I USE THIS? DO ALL/MORE OF THE DO'S AND AVOID THE DON'T'S!

DO'S (READERS COMMENTS):
- GRABS YOU FROM THE FIRST CHAPTER.
- LOVE THE CHARACTERS, PLOT AND CONCLUSION.
- CHARACTERS HAVE A MIXTURE OF PERSONALITIES.
- LOTS OF 'HOLD YOUR BREATH' MOMENTS.
- HEART-STOPPING THEN PULSE-RACING MOMENTS THROUGHOUT.
- THE DIALOGUE AND BANTER THROUGHOUT THIS BOOK IS JUST WONDERFUL INCLUDING SOME BRILLIANTLY FUNNY QUIPS.
- FAST-PACED AND KEPT MY INTEREST.
- THE STORY WAS CHILLING.
- BRILLIANT OPENING CHAPTER, I WAS HOOKED.
- ASTONISHING REVEAL AT THE END.
- AUTHOR GIVES DESCRIPTIONS OF THE AREAS AND HAS YOU WALKING AROUND THEM.
- THE STORY CERTAINLY TORE AT MY HEARTSTRINGS.
- I DOUBT IF YOU WILL SEE THE TWIST IN THE TAIL COMING.
- VERY ACCOMPLISHED WRITING AND PLOTTING WITH A VARIED AND INTERESTING CAST OF CHARACTERS.
- LEFT ME WANTING MORE.
- DIALOGUE WAS AUTHENTIC.
- MAIN CHARACTER HAS MORE THAN HIS FAIR SHARE OF PERSONAL ISSUES.
- GREAT LEVEL OF DETAIL OF CHARACTERS AND SCENERY.
- MADE ME FEEL PART OF THE STORY.
- HAD ME GUESSING ALL THE WAY.
- I INSTANTLY LIKED HIM (THE MAIN CHARACTER).
- CHARACTERS EACH HAVE THEIR OWN VOICES.
- IT IS TRULY ADDICTIVE AND I GOT INTO THE CHARACTERS.
- I COULD VISUALISE THE SCENERY AND ALMOST HEAR THE CHARACTERS' ACCENTS.
- PLENTY OF BELIEVABLE TWISTS AND TURNS.
- A BLEND OF REAL HUMOUR.
- ACCURATE POLICE PROCEDURAL NOVELS.

GENRE BUNDLE: CRIME

NOTE: THIS BUNDLE CAN ALSO INCLUDE THRILLER, MYSTERY, PSYCHOLOGICAL AND HORROR FICTION.

DO'S AND DON'T'S FOR THIS GENRE

HOW CAN I USE THIS? DO ALL/MORE OF THE DO'S AND AVOID THE DON'T'S!

DON'T'S (READERS COMMENTS):
- NO PLOT TWIST.
- POORLY THOUGHT OUT ENDING.
- UNBELIEVABLE PLOT, POORLY CONSTRUCTED, BOGUS TRITE 'TWIST' TACKED ON. AVOID!
- FRUSTRATED BY THE ENDING.
- STEREOTYPICAL/PREDICTABLE.
- CHARACTERS WERE NOT DEVELOPED WELL.
- SO MANY HOLES IN IT AND THE ENDING WAS PREPOSTEROUS.
- STORYTELLING WAS ALL OVER THE PLACE.
- WASN'T A SINGLE LIKEABLE CHARACTER.
- THE CHARACTERS WERE VERY 2-DIMENSIONAL.
- BADLY THOUGHT OUT RED HERRINGS.
- I BEGAN TO LOSE INTEREST.
- IT WAS OVERLY WORDY.
- TOO MANY CHARACTERS TO KEEP TRACK OF.
- CONFUSED PLOTTING.
- I FOUND IT ALL A BIT UNBELIEVABLE.
- I FOUND IT DULL.
- LITTLE SEEDS THAT THE AUTHOR HAD SOWN IN THE NOVEL JUST WENT TOTALLY IGNORED/UNRESOLVED.
- GOT REALLY STRANGE AND WAS SO SLOW.
- TOO MANY CHARACTERS, COULDN'T KEEP TRACK OF EVERYONE.
- I READ UP TO 25% AND NOTHING HAPPENED.
- DRAGGED ON FOR TOO LONG WITH TOO LITTLE GOING ON.
- DIFFICULT TO WORK OUT WHO WAS SAYING WHAT AND WHY.
- STORY WAS TEDIOUS.
- BOOK WAS WRITTEN IT SEEMED IN A RUSH.
- THE LAYOUT WAS A BIT ALL OVER THE PLACE.

BUILD-A-BOOK

GENRE BUNDLE: CRIME

NOTE: THIS BUNDLE CAN ALSO INCLUDE THRILLER, MYSTERY, PSYCHOLOGICAL AND HORROR FICTION.

BOOK COVERS: THIS GENRE USES MAINLY MYSTERIOUS SETTINGS, DARK BLUE/BLACK/RED COLOURS, AND EASY TO READ, STRAIGHTFORWARD FONTS. IT'S MUCH BETTER FOR YOUR BOOK TO BLEND IN AMONGST THE BEST SELLERS, AS THEN YOUR READER WILL BELIEVE YOU BELONG THERE - WHICH YOU DO!

HOW CAN I USE THIS? ENSURE YOUR QUALITY FITS IN WITH THE GENRE AND DOESN'T STAND OUT AS BEING AGAINST WHAT THE READER EXPECTS OF THIS GENRE.

#1
Her Final Words
› Brianna Labuskes
★★★★★ 17
Kindle Edition
£3.29

#2
Trust No One (Devlin & Falco Book 1)
› Debra Webb
★★★★★ 14
Kindle Edition
£3.29

#3
The Late Show
› Michael Connelly
★★★★★ 5,149
Kindle Edition
£0.99

#4
A Place of Execution
› Val McDermid
★★★★★ 394
Kindle Edition
£0.99

#5
The House Guest
› Mark Edwards
★★★★★ 281
Kindle Edition
£3.29

#6
I Found You: From the number one bestselling...
› Lisa Jewell
★★★★★ 1,244
Kindle Edition
£0.99

GENRE BUNDLE: CRIME

NOTE: THIS BUNDLE CAN ALSO INCLUDE THRILLER, MYSTERY, PSYCHOLOGICAL AND HORROR FICTION.

MAIN EMOTION/VIBE OF THE GENRE: DARK, FEAR, SCARED, DEVASTATION AND TERROR.

HOW CAN I USE THIS? ENSURE YOUR READER 'FEELS' THIS EMOTION WITHIN YOUR WRITING USING THE POWER WORDS OR MOST USED WORDS.

IMAGES ASSOCIATED WITH THIS GENRE:

GENRE BUNDLE: CRIME

NOTE: THIS BUNDLE CAN ALSO INCLUDE THRILLER, MYSTERY, PSYCHOLOGICAL AND HORROR FICTION.

WHAT DO WE HAVE NOW? AN AMAZING PLAN!

TITLE (USING THE FORMULA OF 3 WORDS EVOKING QUESTIONS): THE BEST FRIEND; THE TALKING WALLS; THE SILENT VOICE; THE COTTAGE LIE; SECRETS WITHIN WALLS.

A YOUNG GIRL IS REPORTED MISSING BY HER BEST FRIEND.
THE POLICE INVESTIGATE WHAT LOOKS TO NOW BE A MURDER.
THE BEST FRIEND COMES FROM A PERFECT FAMILY AND WHEN DCI THOMAS STARTS WATCHING THE FAMILY MORE CLOSELY, NOT EVERYTHING IS AS IT SEEMS...

MY CHARACTERS ARE CALLED:
SOPHIE: (THE YOUNG GIRL GONE MISSING), 12 YEARS OLD.
ALICE: THE BEST FRIEND, 13 YEARS OLD.
MEG: THE MOTHER OF THE BEST FRIEND HAS A DRINK PROBLEM.
BEN: THE FATHER OF THE BEST FRIEND IS A CONSTRUCTION WORKER.
DCI TOM NICHOLS: DETECTIVE LOOKING INTO IT.

EVENT: IT IS AT THE YOUNG GIRL'S FUNERAL THAT DCI TOM NICHOLS NOTICES THAT THE MOTHER OF THE BEST FRIEND IS ACTING SUSPICIOUSLY.

LOCATIONS: THE FAMILY LIVE IN AN ISOLATED COTTAGE ON THE OUTSKIRTS OF A TOWN.
POWER WORDS: DISTURBING, CHILLING, SECRETS, SILENCE, SLEEPING, MISSING, SUSPECT, MYSTERY, VICTIM, ISOLATED, SHADOWS.

CRIME BOOKS – DO'S AND DON'T'S

WHAT TO DO

We went through all of the reviews from the bestselling crime/mystery/horror and psychological books on Amazon.

We made notes on what reviewers liked and didn't like about that particular book.

We made an easy-to-read table for you (over the page).

If you focus on doing as many of the 'Do's' as possible and limit the 'Don'ts', you're on your way to writing an awesome book your readers will love!

If you want to write in a different genre, we have left space for you to add your findings.

CRIME BOOKS – DO'S AND DON'T'S

DO'S

- "GRABS YOU FROM THE FIRST CHAPTER."

- "MAKE YOUR READERS LOVE THE CHARACTERS, PLOT AND CONCLUSION."

- "CHARACTERS HAVE A MIXTURE OF PERSONALITIES."

- "INCLUDES LOTS OF 'HOLD YOUR BREATH' MOMENTS."

- "HEART-STOPPING THEN PULSE-RACING MOMENTS THROUGHOUT."

- "KEEP DIALOGUE AND BANTER THROUGHOUT THE BOOK ENTERTAINING AND INCLUDE 'BRILLIANTLY FUNNY QUIPS'."

- "KEEP YOUR STORY FAST-PACED AND HOLD THE READER'S INTEREST."

- "THE STORY WAS CHILLING."

- "BRILLIANT OPENING CHAPTER, I WAS HOOKED!"

- "ASTONISHING REVEAL AT THE END."

DON'T'S

- "NO PLOT TWIST."

- "POORLY THOUGHT OUT ENDING."

- "UNBELIEVABLE PLOT, POORLY CONSTRUCTED NARRATIVE, BOGUS TRITE TWIST TACKED ON."

- "MAKE YOUR READERS FRUSTRATED BY THE ENDING."

- "CHARACTERS NOT DEVELOPED WELL."

- "AVOID HOLES IN THE PLOT AND PREPOSTEROUS ENDINGS."

- "STORYTELLING WAS ALL OVER THE PLACE."

- "WASN'T A SINGLE LIKEABLE CHARACTER."

- "THE CHARACTERS WERE VERY 2-DIMENSIONAL."

CRIME BOOKS – DO'S AND DON'T'S

DO'S

- "AUTHOR GIVES DESCRIPTIONS OF THE AREAS AND HAS YOU WALKING THEM."

- "WELL-ROUNDED CHARACTERS."

- "THE STORY CERTAINLY TORE AT MY HEARTSTRINGS."

- "I DOUBT IF YOU WILL SEE THE TWIST IN THE TAIL COMING."

- "VERY ACCOMPLISHED WRITING AND PLOTTING WITH A VARIED AND INTERESTING CAST OF CHARACTERS."

- "LEFT ME WANTING MORE."

- "DIALOGUE WAS AUTHENTIC."

- "MAIN CHARACTER HAS MORE THAN HIS FAIR SHARE OF PERSONAL ISSUES."

- "GREAT LEVEL OF DETAIL OF CHARACTERS AND SCENERY."

- "MADE ME FEEL PART OF THE STORY."

DON'T'S

- "BADLY THOUGHT OUT RED HERRINGS."

- "I BEGAN TO LOSE INTEREST."

- "IT WAS OVERWORKED."

- "TOO MANY CHARACTERS TO KEEP TRACK OF."

- "CONFUSED PLOTTING."

- "FOUND IT ALL A BIT UNBELIEVABLE."

- "I FOUND IT DULL."

- "LITTLE SEEDS THAT THE AUTHOR HAD SOWN IN THE NOVEL JUST WENT TOTALLY IGNORED OR UNRESOLVED."

- "STORY GOT REALLY STRANGE AND WAS SO SLOW."

- "I READ UP TO 25% AND NOTHING HAPPENED."

CRIME BOOKS – DO'S AND DON'T'S

DO'S

- "HAD ME GUESSING ALL THE WAY."

- "I INSTANTLY LIKED HIM (THE MAIN CHARACTER)."

- "CHARACTERS EACH HAVE THEIR OWN VOICES."

- "IT IS TRULY ADDICTIVE AND I GOT INTO THE CHARACTERS."

- "I COULD VISUALISE THE SCENERY AND ALMOST HEAR THE CHARACTERS' ACCENTS."

- "PLENTY OF BELIEVABLE TWISTS AND TURNS."

- "A BLEND OF REAL HUMOUR."

- "ACCURATE POLICE PROCEDURAL NOVELS."

DON'T'S

- "DRAGGED ON FOR TOO LONG WITH TOO LITTLE GOING ON."

- "DIFFICULT TO WORK OUT WHO IS SAYING WHAT AND WHY."

- "STORY WAS TEDIOUS."

- "BOOK WAS WRITTEN, IT SEEMED, IN A RUSH."

- "THE LAYOUT WAS A BIT ALL OVER THE PLACE."

OTHER GENRES – DO'S AND DON'T'S

DO'S

DON'T'S

ENDINGS

WHAT TO DO

HAVE A THINK OF HOW YOU CAN MAKE YOUR READERS GO 'WOW! I WASN'T EXPECTING THAT!'

HAVE AN IDEA OF WHAT YOUR READERS COULD EXPECT, THEN TURN IT UP A NOTCH OR TWO!

SCRIBBLE DOWN ALL POSSIBILITIES. DON'T EDIT.

HAVE FUN!

ENDINGS

HAPPY ENDING:

> THE MAIN CHARACTER ACHIEVES THEIR GOAL (WHAT YOU WOULD HAVE WRITTEN IN THE CHARACTER DESCRIPTIONS) AND 'EVERYBODY IS HAPPY' - FEEL GOOD ENDING.

SAD ENDING:

> TRAGEDY. YOUR MAIN CHARACTER FAILS AT THEIR MISSION, PEOPLE DIE AND EVERYTHING 'GOES WRONG' - WHAT HAPPENS THEN?

THE MAIN CHARACTER ACHIEVES THEIR MISSION:

> BUT IT DOESN'T END HOW THEY WANTED. WHY?

THE CHARACTER FAILS AT THE MISSION:

> BUT LEARNS WHAT THEY NEEDED TO LEARN ABOUT THEMSELVES (USE YOUR DESCRIPTIONS FOR THIS) - WHAT HAPPENS?

ENDINGS

FULL CIRCLE:

BRING THE READERS BACK TO THE SETTING/SITUATION THAT YOU STARTED AT. BUT WHAT'S CHANGED? HAS THE MAIN CHARACTER LEARNED THEIR 'INNER LESSON'?

THE BIG SHOCK!

MAKE SOMETHING HAPPEN THAT IS SO SHOCKING THAT EVERYBODY GOES "WOW!" WHAT COULD BE THE COMPLETE OPPOSITE IDEA BE TO WHAT YOUR READERS WOULD GUESS?

THE CLIFFHANGER:

MAKES YOUR READERS WANT YOUR NEXT BOOK NOW! CREATE INTRIGUE WHERE YOU DON'T QUITE ANSWER A QUESTION BUT 'LEAVE IT HANGING.'

FUNNY/HUMOUROUS ENDING:

FEEL GOOD ENDING - THINK OF YOUR CHARACTERS QUIRKS/TRAITS.

ENDINGS

HIGHLY EMOTIONAL ENDING:

PULL ON YOUR READERS' HEARTSTRINGS. IT COULD BE HAPPY, SAD, TRAGIC ETC... WHAT DO THEY CARE ABOUT AT THIS POINT?

REFLECTION:

THE MAIN CHARACTER HAS LEARNED THEIR LESSONS AND HAS GROWN FROM THE EXPERIENCE AND DOES GOOD WITH IT (CHARACTER ARC).

QUOTE:

MAYBE A QUOTE THAT YOUR CHARACTER SAID AT THE BEGINNING OR SOMETHING THEY LIVE BY NOW MAKES SENSE AND THEY SAY AS THE LAST FEW WORDS WHERE IT HAS MORE MEANING.

YOUR CHARACTER'S WORST FEARS COME TRUE.

YOUR CHARACTER FAILS THEIR MISSION BUT BECOMES A HERO TO EVERYBODY.

YOUR MAIN CHARACTER DISCOVERS SOMETHING MASSIVE ABOUT THEMSELVES.

ENDINGS

WHAT TO DO NOW:

PICK 2-3 IDEAS THAT YOU LIKE:

ROTATE DIFFERENT COMBINATIONS OF YOUR CHARACTERS INTO EACH SCENARIO TO FIND OUT WHICH ONE IS THE MOST EXCITING:

IDEA #1

ENDING SCENARIO:

WHAT DO I WANT THE READER TO FEEL ABOUT THIS ENDING AND WHY?

WHAT DO I NEED TO MAKE SURE I INCLUDE IN THE STORY TO ENSURE THIS ENDING COMES OFF?

ENDINGS

IDEA #2

ENDING SCENARIO:

WHAT DO I WANT THE READER TO FEEL ABOUT THIS ENDING AND WHY?

WHAT DO I NEED TO MAKE SURE I INCLUDE IN THE STORY TO ENSURE THIS ENDING COMES OFF?

ENDINGS

IDEA #3

ENDING SCENARIO:

WHAT DO I WANT THE READER TO FEEL ABOUT THIS ENDING AND WHY?

WHAT DO I NEED TO MAKE SURE I INCLUDE IN THE STORY TO ENSURE THIS ENDING COMES OFF?

HOW MANY CHARACTERS WILL I NEED?

WHAT TO DO

FILL IN THE BLANKS.

THESE ARE OUR SUGGESTIONS WITH HOW MANY CHARACTERS WE THINK ARE A GOOD STARTING POINT.

DEPENDING ON YOUR STORY, YOU MAY NEED MORE OR LESS.

WE HAVE HELPED YOU BY INCLUDING SOME CHARACTER 'TRAITS AND QUIRKS' IN THIS WORKBOOK.

HOW MANY CHARACTERS WILL I NEED?

MAIN CHARACTER (PROTAGONIST)

NAME:

TRAITS?

ALLY

NAME?

TRAITS?

ANTAGONIST

NAME?

TRAITS?

HOW MANY CHARACTERS WILL I NEED?

ALLY OF ANTAGONIST

NAME:

TRAITS?

SOMEBODY TO SAVE (VICTIM)

NAME?

TRAITS?

CONFIDENTE OF MAIN CHARACTER (THE VOICE OF REASON)

NAME?

TRAITS?

HOW MANY CHARACTERS WILL I NEED?

CHARACTER TRAITS

GENEROUS	DISRESPECTFUL	AFFECTIONATE
HAS INTEGRITY	GREEDY	FUNNY
LOYAL	ABRASIVE	ROUGH
DEVOTED	PESSIMIST	TALKATIVE
LOVING	CRUEL	ROWDY
KIND	NARCISSIST	SMART
SINCERE	OBNOXIOUS	FIDGETY
HAS SELF-CONTROL	MALICIOUS	SHY
IS PEACEFUL	PETTY	LIVELY
IS FAITHFUL	SELFISH	PATIENT
HAS PATIENCE	UNFORGIVING	STUBBORN
IS DETERMINED	DOMINANT	COURAGEOUS
PERSISTENT	CONFIDENT	STRONG
ADVENTUROUS	CHARISMATIC	FEARLESS
IS FAIR	BOLD	DARING
CO-OPERATIVE	BORING	BRAVE
TOLERANT	PROACTIVE	WITTY
OPTIMISTIC	ENTHUSIASTIC	INTENSE
SPIRITUAL	EXUDES AUTHORITY	EVIL
DISHONEST	PLAYFUL	CUNNING
DISLOYAL	ACTIVE	MURDEROUS
MEAN	WILD	IMMORAL
RUDE	SILLY	VENGEFUL

CHARACTERS PART 1

MAIN CHARACTER NAME: ....

- DOMINANT TRAIT?

- ONE EXAMPLE OF WHAT THIS TRAIT LOOKS LIKE:

- WHAT WOULD BE AN OPPOSITE TRAIT TO THIS?

- WHAT DOES THIS TRAIT LOOK LIKE?

CHARACTERS PART 1

ALLY TO MAIN CHARACTER NAME: ....

- DOMINANT TRAIT?

- ONE EXAMPLE OF WHAT THIS TRAIT LOOKS LIKE:

- WHAT WOULD BE AN OPPOSITE TRAIT TO THIS?

- WHAT DOES THIS TRAIT LOOK LIKE?

CHARACTERS PART 1

CONFIDANTE TO MAIN CHARACTER NAME: ....

- DOMINANT TRAIT?

- ONE EXAMPLE OF WHAT THIS TRAIT LOOKS LIKE:

- WHAT WOULD BE AN OPPOSITE TRAIT TO THIS?

- WHAT DOES THIS TRAIT LOOK LIKE?

CHARACTERS PART 1

ANTAGONIST NAME: ....

- DOMINANT TRAIT?

- ONE EXAMPLE OF WHAT THIS TRAIT LOOKS LIKE:

- WHAT WOULD BE AN OPPOSITE TRAIT TO THIS?

- WHAT DOES THIS TRAIT LOOK LIKE?

CHARACTERS PART 1

ALLY TO ANTAGONIST NAME: ....

- DOMINANT TRAIT?

- ONE EXAMPLE OF WHAT THIS TRAIT LOOKS LIKE:

- WHAT WOULD BE AN OPPOSITE TRAIT TO THIS?

- WHAT DOES THIS TRAIT LOOK LIKE?

CHARACTERS PART 2

CHARACTER NAME ....
ARE THEY GOOD OR BAD? ....

IF THEY ARE GOOD, HAVE 2 GOOD TRAITS AND 1 BAD TRAIT.
IF THEY ARE BAD, HAVE 2 BAD TRAITS AND 1 GOOD TRAIT.

DOMINANT TRAIT

GIVE ONE EXAMPLE OF HOW THIS TRAIT COULD BE SHOWN IN YOUR BOOK:

TRAIT 2

GIVE ONE EXAMPLE OF HOW THIS TRAIT COULD BE SHOWN IN YOUR BOOK:

TRAIT 3

GIVE ONE EXAMPLE OF HOW THIS TRAIT COULD BE SHOWN IN YOUR BOOK:

CHARACTERS PART 2

CHARACTER NAME ....
ARE THEY GOOD OR BAD? ....

IF THEY ARE GOOD, HAVE 2 GOOD TRAITS AND 1 BAD TRAIT.
IF THEY ARE BAD, HAVE 2 BAD TRAITS AND 1 GOOD TRAIT.

DOMINANT TRAIT

GIVE ONE EXAMPLE OF HOW THIS TRAIT COULD BE SHOWN IN YOUR BOOK:

TRAIT 2

GIVE ONE EXAMPLE OF HOW THIS TRAIT COULD BE SHOWN IN YOUR BOOK:

TRAIT 3

GIVE ONE EXAMPLE OF HOW THIS TRAIT COULD BE SHOWN IN YOUR BOOK:

CHARACTERS PART 2

CHARACTER NAME ....
ARE THEY GOOD OR BAD? ....

IF THEY ARE GOOD, HAVE 2 GOOD TRAITS AND 1 BAD TRAIT.
IF THEY ARE BAD, HAVE 2 BAD TRAITS AND 1 GOOD TRAIT.

DOMINANT TRAIT

GIVE ONE EXAMPLE OF HOW THIS TRAIT COULD BE SHOWN IN YOUR BOOK:

TRAIT 2

GIVE ONE EXAMPLE OF HOW THIS TRAIT COULD BE SHOWN IN YOUR BOOK:

TRAIT 3

GIVE ONE EXAMPLE OF HOW THIS TRAIT COULD BE SHOWN IN YOUR BOOK:

CHARACTERS PART 2

CHARACTER NAME ....
ARE THEY GOOD OR BAD? ....

IF THEY ARE GOOD, HAVE 2 GOOD TRAITS AND 1 BAD TRAIT.
IF THEY ARE BAD, HAVE 2 BAD TRAITS AND 1 GOOD TRAIT.

DOMINANT TRAIT

GIVE ONE EXAMPLE OF HOW THIS TRAIT COULD BE SHOWN IN YOUR BOOK:

TRAIT 2

GIVE ONE EXAMPLE OF HOW THIS TRAIT COULD BE SHOWN IN YOUR BOOK:

TRAIT 3

GIVE ONE EXAMPLE OF HOW THIS TRAIT COULD BE SHOWN IN YOUR BOOK:

CHARACTERS PART 2

CHARACTER NAME ....
ARE THEY GOOD OR BAD? ....

IF THEY ARE GOOD, HAVE 2 GOOD TRAITS AND 1 BAD TRAIT.
IF THEY ARE BAD, HAVE 2 BAD TRAITS AND 1 GOOD TRAIT.

DOMINANT TRAIT

GIVE ONE EXAMPLE OF HOW THIS TRAIT COULD BE SHOWN IN YOUR BOOK:

TRAIT 2

GIVE ONE EXAMPLE OF HOW THIS TRAIT COULD BE SHOWN IN YOUR BOOK:

TRAIT 3

GIVE ONE EXAMPLE OF HOW THIS TRAIT COULD BE SHOWN IN YOUR BOOK:

CHARACTER QUIRKS

WHAT TO DO:

WRITE YOUR CHARACTER NAMES IN THE SPACES.

THERE IS ONE PAGE PER CHARACTER.

IF YOU NEED SOME IDEAS FOR QUIRKS, AT THE END OF THIS CHAPTER, WE HAVE MADE A LIST OF QUIRKS FOR YOU.

TRY AND SPRINKLE SOME UNUSUAL ONES!

CHARACTER QUIRKS

DON'T OVERUSE THESE. EACH CHARACTER SHOULD HAVE 1-2 QUIRKS TO KEEP THEM INTERESTING.

CHARACTER NAME? ....

QUIRK 1:

WHY IS THIS RELEVANT TO MY CHARACTER?

CAN YOU THINK OF A SCENE WHERE THIS CAN BE USED? SHOW DON'T TELL!:

QUIRK 2:

WHY IS THIS RELEVANT TO MY CHARACTER?

CAN YOU THINK OF A SCENE WHERE THIS CAN BE USED? SHOW DON'T TELL!:

CHARACTER QUIRKS

DON'T OVERUSE THESE. EACH CHARACTER SHOULD HAVE 1-2 QUIRKS TO KEEP THEM INTERESTING.

CHARACTER NAME? ....

QUIRK 1:

WHY IS THIS RELEVANT TO MY CHARACTER?

CAN YOU THINK OF A SCENE WHERE THIS CAN BE USED? SHOW DON'T TELL!:

QUIRK 2:

WHY IS THIS RELEVANT TO MY CHARACTER?

CAN YOU THINK OF A SCENE WHERE THIS CAN BE USED? SHOW DON'T TELL!:

CHARACTER QUIRKS

DON'T OVERUSE THESE. EACH CHARACTER SHOULD HAVE 1-2 QUIRKS TO KEEP THEM INTERESTING.

CHARACTER NAME? ....

QUIRK 1:

WHY IS THIS RELEVANT TO MY CHARACTER?

CAN YOU THINK OF A SCENE WHERE THIS CAN BE USED? SHOW DON'T TELL!:

QUIRK 2:

WHY IS THIS RELEVANT TO MY CHARACTER?

CAN YOU THINK OF A SCENE WHERE THIS CAN BE USED? SHOW DON'T TELL!:

CHARACTER QUIRKS

DON'T OVERUSE THESE. EACH CHARACTER SHOULD HAVE 1-2 QUIRKS TO KEEP THEM INTERESTING.

CHARACTER NAME? ....

QUIRK 1:

WHY IS THIS RELEVANT TO MY CHARACTER?

CAN YOU THINK OF A SCENE WHERE THIS CAN BE USED? SHOW DON'T TELL!:

QUIRK 2:

WHY IS THIS RELEVANT TO MY CHARACTER?

CAN YOU THINK OF A SCENE WHERE THIS CAN BE USED? SHOW DON'T TELL!:

CHARACTER QUIRKS

DON'T OVERUSE THESE. EACH CHARACTER SHOULD HAVE 1-2 QUIRKS TO KEEP THEM INTERESTING.

CHARACTER NAME? ....

QUIRK 1:

WHY IS THIS RELEVANT TO MY CHARACTER?

CAN YOU THINK OF A SCENE WHERE THIS CAN BE USED? SHOW DON'T TELL!:

QUIRK 2:

WHY IS THIS RELEVANT TO MY CHARACTER?

CAN YOU THINK OF A SCENE WHERE THIS CAN BE USED? SHOW DON'T TELL!:

CHARACTER QUIRKS

DON'T OVERUSE THESE. EACH CHARACTER SHOULD HAVE 1-2 QUIRKS TO KEEP THEM INTERESTING.

CHARACTER NAME? ....

QUIRK 1:

WHY IS THIS RELEVANT TO MY CHARACTER?

CAN YOU THINK OF A SCENE WHERE THIS CAN BE USED? SHOW DON'T TELL!:

QUIRK 2:

WHY IS THIS RELEVANT TO MY CHARACTER?

CAN YOU THINK OF A SCENE WHERE THIS CAN BE USED? SHOW DON'T TELL!:

CHARACTER QUIRKS

IF YOU ARE STUCK FOR IDEAS, CONSIDER PICKING SOME FROM THIS LIST:

- VERY INTROVERTED, QUIET AND RESERVED, KEEPS TO THEMSELVES.
- HIGHLY EXTROVERTED, LOVES SOCIALISING AND MEETING NEW PEOPLE.
- A MEGA CONTROL FREAK WHO HAS TO HAVE EVERYTHING THEIR WAY.
- NEAT FREAK (OFTEN COINCIDES WITH CONTROL FREAK).
- TOTAL SLOB WHO NEVER KNOWS WHERE ANYTHING IS.
- SUPER STUBBORN AND WILL NEVER ADMIT WHEN THEY'RE WRONG.
- BRUTALLY HONEST AND CAN'T LIE TO SAVE THEIR LIFE.
- EXTREMELY JUDGEMENTAL OF OTHER PEOPLE.
- SHORT-TEMPERED, ESPECIALLY WHEN IRRITATED.
- ALWAYS PATIENT, EVEN WHEN FRUSTRATED.
- HILARIOUS OR ODD SENSE OF HUMOUR.
- VERY HARD TO MAKE THEM LAUGH.
- LOVES TO EAT AND IS OBSESSED WITH FOOD.

CHARACTER QUIRKS

IF YOU ARE STUCK FOR IDEAS, CONSIDER PICKING SOME FROM THIS LIST:

LOVES TO DRINK AND IS CONSTANTLY PARTYING.

CONSTANTLY COMPLAINS ABOUT EVERYTHING.

EXTREMELY LOYAL AND WILL DO ANYTHING FOR FRIENDS/FAMILY.

ADVENTUROUS AND WILLING TO TRY ANYTHING.

CAUTIOUS AND CAREFUL NO MATTER WHAT.

ENERGETIC, HARDLY EVER NEEDS TO REST.

SLEEPS ALL THE TIME AND STILL GETS TIRED DURING THE DAY.

A HORRIBLE SENSE OF DIRECTION AND CONSTANTLY GETS LOST.

AN OVERACHIEVER WHO LOVES SCHOOL/STRUCTURE.

REALLY MODEST AND WON'T EVER BRAG ABOUT THEMSELVES.

EXTREMELY EMOTIONAL AND WILL CRY AT THE DROP OF A HAT.

STOIC AND DETACHED, RARELY SHOWS EMOTION.

WILDCARD WHOSE BEHAVIOUR IS UNPREDICTABLE, EVEN TO FRIENDS.

CHARACTER QUIRKS

IF YOU ARE STUCK FOR IDEAS, CONSIDER PICKING SOME FROM THIS LIST:

NOTORIOUSLY TWO-FACED AND WILL BETRAY ANYONE.

CHARISMATIC AND CAN CONVINCE ANYONE TO DO THEIR BIDDING.

VERY PROPER AND ALWAYS POLITE TO OTHERS.

DATES TONS OF PEOPLE & HAS A NEW BOY/GIRLFRIEND EVERY WEEK.

OBSESSIVE PERSONALITY — WHETHER IT'S A TV SHOW, BRAND, MUSICAL ARTIST, OR EVEN ANOTHER PERSON, THEY'LL GET ATTACHED AND THINK/TALK ABOUT IT CONSTANTLY.

FANTASTIC COOK OR BAKER.

SKILLED MUSICIAN (PIANO, GUITAR, VIOLIN, ETC.).

ARTISTIC TALENT (DRAWING, PAINTING, SCULPTING, ETC.).

MODEL ATHLETE (FOOTBALL, HOCKEY, SWIMMING, ETC.).

GREAT AT VOICES/VENTRILOQUY.

CAN DO SLEIGHT-OF-HAND — MAY BE A PICKPOCKET.

SPEAKS MULTIPLE LANGUAGES, EVEN OBSCURE ONES.

CHARACTER QUIRKS

IF YOU ARE STUCK FOR IDEAS, CONSIDER PICKING SOME FROM THIS LIST:

KNOWS EVERYTHING ABOUT HISTORY.

MATHEMATICAL OR SCIENTIFIC GENIUS.

BRILLIANT CODER AND CAN HACK INTO ANY DATABASE.

SKILLED MECHANICAL INVENTOR.

CAN BUILD OR PUT TOGETHER ANYTHING.

SUPER-QUICK LOGICAL REASONING.

EXCEPTIONAL MEMORY/GENIUS IQ (SEVERAL OF THE ABOVE MIGHT FALL UNDER THIS ONE).

SPECIAL CONNECTION WITH ANIMALS.

SUPER EMPATHETIC AND UNDERSTANDING OF OTHER PEOPLE.

EXTREMELY FAST RUNNER.

CONTORTIONIST (CAN TWIST THEIR BODY INTO ANY SHAPE).

PSYCHIC TALENT (CAN PREDICT THE FUTURE).

AMAZING MECHANIC.

CHARACTER QUIRKS

IF YOU ARE STUCK FOR IDEAS, CONSIDER PICKING SOME FROM THIS LIST:

SUPER STRENGTH, FLYING, INVISIBILITY OR OTHER SUPERPOWERS.

UNUSUALLY HIGH TOLERANCE FOR PAIN.

SURVIVAL SKILLS LIKE HUNTING AND FISHING.

QUICK REFLEXES, ACTS FAST IN A CRISIS.

BRAVE AND FEARLESS, NOT SCARED OF ANYTHING.

ABLE TO TALK THEIR WAY OUT OF ANY TROUBLE/INVENT STORIES ON THE FLY.

CHARACTER QUIRKS

WEAKNESSES/NEGATIVE TRAITS:

Awful driver.

Always running late.

Illegible handwriting.

Terrible at public speaking.

Socially awkward — hard for them to make friends.

Has tons of credit card debt from online shopping.

Self-destructive and always wants what's worst for them.

Gets blackout drunk every time they go out.

Extremely conceited or arrogant.

Compulsive liar.

Manipulative of friends.

Gets jealous over nothing.

Often mean for no reason.

CHARACTER QUIRKS

WEAKNESSES/NEGATIVE TRAITS:

UNBELIEVABLY SELF-CENTRED.

EXTREMELY PASSIVE-AGGRESSIVE.

ARACHNOPHOBIA (AN IRRATIONAL FEAR OF SPIDERS).

COULROPHOBIA (AN IRRATIONAL FEAR OF CLOWNS).

AGORAPHOBIA (AN IRRATIONAL FEAR OF LEAVING THE HOUSE).

PANTOPHOBIA (FEAR OF EVERYTHING).

DRESSES ALL IN ONE COLOUR

BEDROOM IS DECORATED EXACTLY LIKE A PINTEREST PICTURE

WON'T DRINK STILL WATER, ONLY SPARKLING

REFUSES TO USE HEADPHONES AND BLASTS THEIR MUSIC IN PUBLIC

ALWAYS DRESSES TOO NICELY FOR THE OCCASION

WALKS AROUND BAREFOOT, EVEN IN STORES AND OTHER PUBLIC PLACES

HATES BEING INSIDE, SLEEPS AND GOES TO THE BATHROOM OUTDOORS

CHARACTER QUIRKS

WEAKNESSES/NEGATIVE TRAITS:

Can't help but look in every mirror they pass.

Wears a small plastic backpack everywhere.

Preps their meals three weeks in advance.

Drinks shots of espresso all day long.

Sings opera in the shower.

Makes their own (terrible) abstract art and hangs it on their walls.

Gets super excited about Christmas and then really depressed in January.

Refuses to wear glasses even though they need them.

Carries around a secret teddy bear.

Has been wearing the same friendship bracelet for three years.

Fastidiously lint-rolls all their clothing.

Will leave a shop or restaurant if someone walks in with a baby.

CHARACTER QUIRKS

WEAKNESSES/NEGATIVE TRAITS:

Extremely superstitious (knocks on wood/avoids number 13).

Drops everything other people ask them to hold.

Likes to go out dancing by themselves.

Prefers to have the lights off or dimmed at all times.

Only reads books written before 1900.

Only watches movies that get really bad reviews.

Always wears multiple sweaters on top of each other.

Won't eat anything that doesn't have bread (at least on the side).

Thinks they're a time-traveller from the medieval era.

Gives friends and family excellent homemade presents.

Leaves the office last every day so they can push all the chairs in.

Hates jagged numbers (always fills their gas tank to the pound, sends emails on the hour, etc.).

CHARACTER QUIRKS

WEAKNESSES/NEGATIVE TRAITS:

Has an imaginary friend they still talk to, even in adulthood.

Owns a lizard that they try and use as a guard dog.

Listens exclusively to Britney Spears.

Leaves little notes in library books for future readers.

Uses tissues to hold onto poles on public transportation.

Wears their hair in Princess Leia buns.

Never goes a day without talking to their mum.

Hums "In the Hall of the Mountain King" when they get stressed.

Clicks their tongue while walking, so they sound like a horse.

Quotes Pulp Fiction all the time.

Loves hanging out in completely empty places.

Convinced they're going to die in a freak accident.

CHARACTER QUIRKS

WEAKNESSES/NEGATIVE TRAITS:

Grows all their own food in their vegetable garden.

Never pays for train or bus tickets.

Can recite Shakespearean sonnets.

Recycles and eats vegetarian, but only out of guilt.

Has a "vision board" posted on their ceiling.

Loves the beach but hates swimming.

Flicks people in the forehead when they get annoyed.

Laughs at everything, even bad jokes.

Curates a great Instagram feed of street art.

CHARACTER QUIRKS

CLICHED "QUIRKS" TO AVOID:

PALE SKIN.

CROOKED SMILE.

"INTENSE" STARE.

RELENTLESS CLUMSINESS.

ARTIFICIAL HAIR COLOURS THAT ARE SUPPOSEDLY NATURAL.

CHARACTERS THINKING THEY'RE UNATTRACTIVE WHEN EVERYONE ELSE THINKS THEY'RE BEAUTIFUL.

Credit: https://blog.reedsy.com/character-quirks/

CHARACTER QUIRKS

CLICHED "QUIRKS" TO AVOID:

WINKS AT PARTICULAR CHARACTERS: AN AMOROUS OR OBSESSED INDIVIDUAL.

SCOFFS AS A VICTORIAN GENTLEMAN: "HARUMPH" BY A SNOBBY HIGH CLASS FELLOW.

HIGH PITCHED VOICE: A YOUNG PERSON OR EUNUCH.

CONSTANTLY RUBS HANDS: NERVOUS OR OVERLY CLEANLY PERSON.

SPEAKS SLOWLY: OLD OR STEADY-GOING PERSON.

TWIRLS MOUSTACHE/HAIR: SOMEONE WHO IS EASILY BORED OR OVERTLY EVIL.

GIVES NICKNAMES TO PEOPLE: CALLS PEOPLE BY HAIR COLOUR OR OTHER FEATURE.

PICKS NOSE/EARS OFTEN: A YOUNG OR HABITUAL PERSON.

SCRATCHES BUTT: AN UNCOUTH PERSON.

REFUSES LOW-QUALITY FOOD: SOMEONE WITH A FEAR OF GERMS OR RICH PERSON.

Credit: https://media.spokesman.com/documents/2015/07/quirks_5fa8l0K.pdf

CHARACTER QUIRKS

CLICHED "QUIRKS" TO AVOID:

CONSTANTLY USES HANDS WHEN TALKING: A SALESPERSON OR SOMEONE WHO LIKES TO EXAGGERATE.

RUBS EYES AND FOREHEAD: A PERSON WHO DOES NOT SLEEP VERY WELL/OFTEN.

ANIMAL LOVER: HAS A SOFT SPOT FOR ANIMALS.

COMBS HAIR OFTEN: A DAPPER DAN MAN WHO TAKES PRIDE IN THEIR HAIR/BEARD.

CONSTANTLY VULGAR: BARBARIC OR TOUGH INDIVIDUALS.

RANDOM SCRATCHES HEAD: A NERVOUS OR LICE-RIDDEN PERSON.

CRITICISES EVERYTHING: SOMEONE WITH HIGH STANDARDS OR DOESN'T DO A LOT OF WORK.

SNIFFS THINGS/PEOPLE: A SOCIALLY CHALLENGED CREATURE/PERSON WHO LIKES SMELLS.

ADJUSTS CLOTHES/GLASSES: SOMEONE WHO DOESN'T SPEND MONEY ON WELL-FITTING ATTIRE.

Credit: https://media.spokesman.com/documents/2015/07/quirks_5fa8l0K.pdf

CHARACTER QUIRKS

CLICHED "QUIRKS" TO AVOID:

CONSTANTLY CHECKS THE TIME: A NERVOUS BUSINESS PERSON WITH A POCKET WATCH.

DOESN'T TALK: A MUTE OR TOOK A VOW OF SILENCE.

BATHES AT ANY OPPORTUNITY: CLEANLINESS IS A HIGH PRIORITY.

LAIDBACK AND EASY-GOING: A RELAXED OR CONSTANTLY DRUGGED PERSON.

YAWNS: A PERSON WHO CAN'T GET ENOUGH SLEEP.

FORGETFUL: SOMEONE WITH A HEAD INJURY.

GERMAPHOBIC: A PERSON UNCOMFORTABLE AROUND GERMS.

RANDOMLY MAKES NOISES: ROOSTER CALL DURING A DISCUSSION.

SPURTS OUT WORDS SPONTANEOUSLY: COMPLEX TOURETTE'S SYNDROME TICKS.

WAVES WEAPONS AROUND: A PERSON RAISED IN A BARBARIC SOCIETY.

VERY SLOW BLINKING: SOMEONE WHO OFTEN ZONES OUT.

Credit: https://media.spokesman.com/documents/2015/07/quirks_5fa8l0K.pdf

CHARACTER QUIRKS

CLICHED "QUIRKS" TO AVOID:

OVERLY CHIPPER: YOUTHFUL OR NAÏVE PERSON.

SNORTS: SOMEONE WITH NOSE PROBLEMS.

RANDOMLY USES OTHER LANGUAGE(S): A PERSON NEW TO THE COMMON LANGUAGE.

QUICK TO ANGER/OFFENCE: AN ANGRY PERSON, LIKE BARBARIAN OR GANG MEMBER.

SQUINTS EYES: BAD EYESIGHT OR SOMEONE USED TO DARKNESS.

SNAPS FINGERS CONSTANTLY: HAS A NERVOUS TIC OR LIKES JAZZ.

SPEAKS QUICKLY: TOO MANY THOUGHTS THAT NEED TO COME OUT.

GRAVELLY VOICE: GRUFF INDIVIDUAL OR MINER OF SORTS.

THINKS THEY'RE HILARIOUS: THEY LIKE TO LAUGH AT THEIR OWN JOKES.

TWIDDLES FINGERS: ENERGETIC, NERVOUS OR TWITCHY PEOPLE.

NEVER IS WITHOUT FOOD: LARGE CHARACTERS OR JUST SOMEONE WHO LIKES TO EAT.

Credit: https://media.spokesman.com/documents/2015/07/quirks_5faBIOK.pdf

CHARACTER QUIRKS

CLICHED "QUIRKS" TO AVOID:

CLEANS WEAPONS OFTEN: SOMEONE WHO TAKES GREAT PRIDE IN THEIR WEAPONS.

CONSTANTLY DISTRACTED: HAVING TOO MUCH ENERGY OR THINKING TOO MUCH.

REPLACES CURSE WORD(S) WITH OTHERS: FRAK FROM BATTLESTAR GALACTICA, CURSES IN OTHER LANGUAGES.

DEBBY DOWNER: CAN FIND SADNESS IN EVERYTHING.

UNCOMFORTABLE/CREEPY SMILE: MISCHIEVOUS OR EVIL PEOPLE.

ENDS EVERY SENTENCE IN A PHRASE: "HE WAS LIKE TOTALLY, YOU KNOW?" "THEN HE WAS, YOU KNOW?"

YOU'RE YOUR OWN FAVOURITE PERSON: YOU TALK ABOUT YOURSELF A LOT.

MUTTERS MOST OF THE TIME: A SHY, UNCONFIDENT, OR SOFT-SPOKEN PERSON.

OVERLY POLITE: SOMEONE TAUGHT IN THE WAYS OF ETIQUETTE.

Credit: https://media.spokesman.com/documents/2015/07/quirks_5fa8lOK.pdf

CHARACTER QUIRKS

CLICHED "QUIRKS" TO AVOID:

HAS AND USES A CATCHPHRASE: HERO WANNABE OR SOMEONE HUNG UP ON AN IDEA

STEEPLES HANDS DURING CONVERSATION: MR. BURNS OR SOMEONE WHO THINKS A LOT.

DAYDREAMER: YOUNG OR ADVENTUROUS PEOPLE.

RUBS THEIR CHIN/BEARD: THINKERS AND PLOTTERS.

INAPPROPRIATE JOKING: SOMEONE RAISED AWAY FROM SOCIETY.

REFERS TO THE SAME THING, CONSTANTLY: GRANDPA TELLING THE SAME STORIES AGAIN AND AGAIN.

FALLS ASLEEP RANDOMLY: SOMEONE WHO STAYS UP LATE OR SUFFERS NARCOLEPSY.

LEANS ON THINGS AND PEOPLE: A PERSON WITH A LIMP OR WHO WANTS TO BE CLOSE TO OTHERS.

THEY SPEAK WITH AN ACCENT: SOMEONE FROM A DISTANT LAND.

AGGRESSIVE BODY LANGUAGE: THUGS OR STRONG.

Credit: https://media.spokesman.com/documents/2015/07/quirks_5fa8l0K.pdf

CHARACTER QUIRKS

CLICHED "QUIRKS" TO AVOID:

MOUTH HANGS OPEN WHEN NOT TALKING: A PERSON WHO GOES DEEP INTO THOUGHT.

TURNED UP NOSE: SOMEONE OF HIGH CLASS THAT LOOKS DOWN ON PEOPLE.

SPONTANEOUSLY TWITCHES HEAD: A NERVOUS PERSON OR SOMEONE WHO HAS HAD HEAD DAMAGE.

USES COIN IN CONVERSATION CONSTANTLY: SOMEONE WHO FLAUNTS THEIR WEALTH.

ACKNOWLEDGES EVERYONE THEY SEE: FRIENDLY, OUTGOING AND/OR FORGETFUL PERSON.

DEEP VOICE: LARGE AND/OR MENACING PEOPLE.

RARELY LOOKS PEOPLE IN THE FACE: DEPRESSED OR WANTED PERSON.

FLIRTY: ANYONE LOOKING FOR LOVE IN THIS TRYING WORLD OF OURS.

Credit: https://media.spokesman.com/documents/2015/07/quirks_5fa8l0K.pdf

EXTENDED CHARACTER DESCRIPTIONS

WHAT TO DO

Write the name of your main character.

You want to know them inside out.

Fill in the blanks.

Doing this now will help you out when it comes to writing your first draft.

If you do want to do this for more than one character, just copy out the questions and fill in the blanks.

EXTENDED CHARACTER DESCRIPTIONS

- NAME OF CHARACTER/AGE?

NAME:

AGE:

- FAMILY HISTORY/TREE?

- RELATION IN THE STORY/MAIN PART?

- JOB?

EXTENDED CHARACTER DESCRIPTIONS

- BIRTH DATE/STARSIGN?

BIRTH DATE:

STARSIGN:

- WEALTH?

- ACCENT?

- HOBBIES?

EXTENDED CHARACTER DESCRIPTIONS

- STRENGTHS AND HOW THIS IMPACTS THEIR LIFE?

- WEAKNESSES AND HOW THIS IMPACTS THEIR LIFE?

- VULNERABILITIES AND HOW THIS IMPACTS THEIR LIFE?

- FEARS AND HOW THIS IMPACTS THEIR LIFE?

EXTENDED CHARACTER DESCRIPTIONS

- DREAMS AS A CHILD AND HOW THAT IMPACTS THEIR LIFE?

- OBSTACLES TO THAT DREAM AND WHY?

- ACHILLES HEEL AND WHY? WHAT WOULD LITERALLY DEVASTATE THIS CHARACTER?

- CONTRADICTIONS AND WHY?

EXTENDED CHARACTER DESCRIPTIONS

- DISADVANTAGE THE CHARACTER. HOW? WHY?

- MOTIVATIONS IN LIFE AND WHY?

- WHAT DOES THE CHARACTER NEED TO LEARN AND WHY? WHAT HAPPENS IF THEY DON'T?

- HOW DOES THE CHARACTER FEEL ABOUT HAVING TO LEARN THESE THINGS AND WHY?

EXTENDED CHARACTER DESCRIPTIONS

- UNUSUAL TRAITS/QUIRKS AND WHY?

- WHAT DOES THE CHARACTER WANT TO LEARN AND WHY? WHAT HAPPENS IF THEY DON'T AND WHY?

- WHAT IS THE CHARACTER'S MAIN PROBLEM IN LIFE? WHY? HOW DOES THIS IMPACT THEM?

- ACHIEVEMENTS: HOW, WHEN, WHY? HOW DOES THIS IMPACT THEIR LIFE NOW?

EXTENDED CHARACTER DESCRIPTIONS

- WHAT COULD BE THE WORST THING? TO HAPPEN TO THEM IN A SCENE AND WHY? IMPACT?

- WHAT COULD BE THE WORST THING TO HAPPEN TO THEM IN THE STORY AND WHY? IMPACT?

- INTERESTS? IMPACT ON LIFE?

- PET HATES AND WHY? IMPACT?

# EXTENDED CHARACTER DESCRIPTIONS

- SECRETS? WHY/HOW DOES THIS AFFECT THEM? IMPACT?

- WHAT IF THE SECRET GOT EXPOSED AND WHY?

- WHAT MAKES THEM CRY?

- WHAT MAKES THEM ANGRY? WHY? IMPACT?

EXTENDED CHARACTER DESCRIPTIONS

- WHAT MAKES THEM LAUGH? WHY? IMPACT?

- IS THERE ANY URGENCY IN THE STORY? A COUNTDOWN? WHY? IMPACT IF NOT SUCCESSFUL?

- HOW WILL THEY ACT IN ACT 1?

- HOW WILL THEY ACT IN ACT 2?

EXTENDED CHARACTER DESCRIPTIONS

- HOW WILL THEY ACT IN ACT 3?

- ANYTHING UNUSUAL ABOUT THEM?

- WHAT ARE SOME OF THEIR STRONG VALUES IN LIFE AND WHY?

- HOW DO THEY DRESS?

EXTENDED CHARACTER DESCRIPTIONS

- WHAT IS THEIR LEVEL OF PATIENCE WITH THINGS AND WHY?

- WHAT IS THEIR IMMEDIATE THOUGHT WHEN THEY WAKE UP AND WHY?

- WHAT DO THEY DO LAST THING AT NIGHT AND WHY?

- HOW DO THEY FEEL ABOUT THE SUMMER MONTHS AND WHY? WHAT WOULD THEY DO/NOT DO?

EXTENDED CHARACTER DESCRIPTIONS

- HOW DO THEY FEEL ABOUT THE WINTER MONTHS AND WHY? WHAT WOULD THEY DO/NOT DO?

- WHAT WOULD THIS CHARACTER HATE TO HEAR OTHERS SAYING ABOUT THEM AND WHY?

- DOES THIS CHARACTER HAVE A BIG EGO? IF SO, HOW DOES IT SHOW ITSELF? IF NOT, HOW CAN THIS BE SHOWN?

- WHAT DOES THEIR 'NORMAL' DAY LOOK LIKE? ROUTINE, RITUALS? WHAT TIME DO THEY GET UP?

EXTENDED CHARACTER DESCRIPTIONS

- WHAT WOULD BE THE COMPLETE OPPOSITE OF THIS 'NORMAL' DAY? INCLUDE AS MANY THINGS AS YOU CAN.

- WHAT DO THEY SAY THEIR IDEAL DAY LOOKS LIKE AND WHY?

- WHAT DO YOU NEED TO MAKE SURE THIS CHARACTER DOES IN THIS BOOK?

- WHAT EMOTIONS DO YOU WANT THE READER TO FEEL ABOUT THIS CHARACTER AND HOW CAN YOU SHOW THIS?

EXTENDED CHARACTER DESCRIPTIONS

- WHAT WOULD BE THE OPPOSITE EMOTION TO THIS? HOW COULD YOU SHOW THIS?.

- HOW DOES THIS CHARACTER ACT WHEN THINGS ARE GOING THEIR WAY AND WHY? TRAITS? SHOW WHAT THEY DO.

- HOW DOES THIS CHARACTER ACT WHEN THEY FEEL THE WORLD IS AGAINST THEM AND WHY? TRAITS? SHOW WHAT THEY DO.

- HOW DOES THIS CHARACTER ACT WHEN SOMEBODY DISAGREES WITH THEM AND WHY? TRAITS? SHOW WHAT THEY DO.

EXTENDED CHARACTER DESCRIPTIONS

- HOW DOES THIS CHARACTER ACT WHEN THINGS GO WRONG AND WHY? TRAITS? SHOW WHAT THEY DO.

- HOW DOES THIS CHARACTER FEEL ABOUT SEX AND WHY?

- WHAT IS THEIR BEST MEMORY AS A CHILD AND WHY?

- WHAT IS THEIR MOST PAINFUL MEMORY AS A CHILD?

EXTENDED CHARACTER DESCRIPTIONS

- DOES THIS CHARACTER BELIEVE IN REVENGE? IF SO, HOW WOULD THEY GET IT?

- HOW DO THEY ACT IN VICTORY?

CHARACTER FREESTYLE POINTS

CHARACTER NAME: ....

- TELL US ABOUT HIM/HER. HOW WOULD HE/SHE REACT? WHERE WOULD HE/SHE GO ON HOLIDAY? WHAT WOULD HE/SHE TALK ABOUT? WHERE WOULD THEY DO THEIR SHOPPING? WHAT CLOTHES WOULD HE/SHE WEAR? HOW WOULD THEY DRIVE THEIR CAR? HOW POLITE ARE THEY?

CHARACTER FREESTYLE POINTS

CHARACTER NAME: ....

- TELL US ABOUT HIM/HER. HOW WOULD HE/SHE REACT? WHERE WOULD HE/SHE GO ON HOLIDAY? WHAT WOULD HE/SHE TALK ABOUT? WHERE WOULD THEY DO THEIR SHOPPING? WHAT CLOTHES WOULD HE/SHE WEAR? HOW WOULD THEY DRIVE THEIR CAR? HOW POLITE ARE THEY?

CHARACTER FREESTYLE POINTS

CHARACTER NAME: ....

- TELL US ABOUT HIM/HER. HOW WOULD HE/SHE REACT? WHERE WOULD HE/SHE GO ON HOLIDAY? WHAT WOULD HE/SHE TALK ABOUT? WHERE WOULD THEY DO THEIR SHOPPING? WHAT CLOTHES WOULD HE/SHE WEAR? HOW WOULD THEY DRIVE THEIR CAR? HOW POLITE ARE THEY?

CHARACTER FREESTYLE POINTS

CHARACTER NAME: ....

- TELL US ABOUT HIM/HER. HOW WOULD HE/SHE REACT? WHERE WOULD HE/SHE GO ON HOLIDAY? WHAT WOULD HE/SHE TALK ABOUT? WHERE WOULD THEY DO THEIR SHOPPING? WHAT CLOTHES WOULD HE/SHE WEAR? HOW WOULD THEY DRIVE THEIR CAR? HOW POLITE ARE THEY?

CHARACTER ARCS

WHAT TO DO

ACT 1: THE BEGINNING
INTRODUCING MAIN CHARACTERS.
INCITING EVENT.
INTRODUCE THE STORY.

ACT 2: THE MIDDLE
THE CHANGE- CHARACTERS CHANGING.
INTRODUCING THE PROBLEM.

ACT 3: THE END
HOW HAVE CHARACTERS CHANGED?
TYING UP LOOSE ENDS.
END ON A HIGH.

CHARACTER ARCS

CHARACTER NAME ....

ACT 1

HOW WILL THEY ACT?

HOW CAN I SHOW THIS?
(USE CHARACTER DESCRIPTIONS)

ACT 2

HOW WILL THEY ACT?

HOW CAN I SHOW THIS?
(USE CHARACTER DESCRIPTIONS AND INCLUDE FAILURES)

ACT 3

HOW WILL THEY ACT?

HOW CAN I SHOW THIS?
(USE CHARACTER DESCRIPTIONS)

CHARACTER ARCS

CHARACTER NAME ....

ACT 1

HOW WILL THEY ACT?

HOW CAN I SHOW THIS?
(USE CHARACTER DESCRIPTIONS)

ACT 2

HOW WILL THEY ACT?

HOW CAN I SHOW THIS?
(USE CHARACTER DESCRIPTIONS AND INCLUDE FAILURES)

ACT 3

HOW WILL THEY ACT?

HOW CAN I SHOW THIS?
(USE CHARACTER DESCRIPTIONS)

CHARACTER ARCS

CHARACTER NAME ....

ACT 1

HOW WILL THEY ACT?

HOW CAN I SHOW THIS?
(USE CHARACTER DESCRIPTIONS)

ACT 2

HOW WILL THEY ACT?

HOW CAN I SHOW THIS?
(USE CHARACTER DESCRIPTIONS AND INCLUDE FAILURES)

ACT 3

HOW WILL THEY ACT?

HOW CAN I SHOW THIS?
(USE CHARACTER DESCRIPTIONS)

CHARACTER ARCS

CHARACTER NAME ....

ACT 1

HOW WILL THEY ACT?

HOW CAN I SHOW THIS?
(USE CHARACTER DESCRIPTIONS)

ACT 2

HOW WILL THEY ACT?

HOW CAN I SHOW THIS?
(USE CHARACTER DESCRIPTIONS AND INCLUDE FAILURES)

ACT 3

HOW WILL THEY ACT?

HOW CAN I SHOW THIS?
(USE CHARACTER DESCRIPTIONS)

CHARACTER ARCS

CHARACTER NAME ....

ACT 1

HOW WILL THEY ACT?

HOW CAN I SHOW THIS?
(USE CHARACTER DESCRIPTIONS)

ACT 2

HOW WILL THEY ACT?

HOW CAN I SHOW THIS?
(USE CHARACTER DESCRIPTIONS AND INCLUDE FAILURES)

ACT 3

HOW WILL THEY ACT?

HOW CAN I SHOW THIS?
(USE CHARACTER DESCRIPTIONS)

CHARACTER ARCS

CHARACTER NAME ....

ACT 1

HOW WILL THEY ACT?

HOW CAN I SHOW THIS?
(USE CHARACTER DESCRIPTIONS)

ACT 2

HOW WILL THEY ACT?

HOW CAN I SHOW THIS?
(USE CHARACTER DESCRIPTIONS AND INCLUDE FAILURES)

ACT 3

HOW WILL THEY ACT?

HOW CAN I SHOW THIS?
(USE CHARACTER DESCRIPTIONS)

RESEARCH

WHERE DO I GO FOR RESEARCH?

GOOGLE
THIS IS FOR EVERYTHING! LITERALLY, TYPE IN WHAT YOU NEED. EG. 'ARMY UNIFORM SECOND WORLD WAR.'

GOOGLE IMAGES
FOR EVERYTHING TO HELP DESCRIBE FOOD, PLACES, HOUSES ETC...

GOOGLE EARTH/MAPS
GREAT FOR LOCATIONS, ESPECIALLY IF THEY ARE IN A DIFFERENT COUNTRY. LOOK AT STREET VIEW FOR EVEN MORE DETAIL.

ESTATE AGENTS/REALTORS
YOU CAN SEE STREET VIEWS, FLOOR PLANS OF HOUSES IN STREETS YOU WANT TO DESCRIBE. LOTS OF PICTURES AND A LOT OF THE TIME THEY WILL HAVE PICTURES OF IT BEING FULLY FURNISHED TO ADD CHARACTER.

NATIONAL ARCHIVES
AGAIN, GOOGLE THIS AND SELECT WHICH ERA, EVENT ETC. YOU WANT TO RESEARCH. YOU CAN ALSO CONTACT THESE PLACES AND THEY WILL HELP YOU.

RESEARCH

WHERE DO I GO FOR RESEARCH?

SEARCH KEYWORDS ON TWITTER AND INSTAGRAM

FOR EXAMPLE #POLICEOFFICER #ARMYUNIFORM #TUDORHOUSE #MEXICANFOOD #DOCTOR

THIS IS LIKELY TO BRING UP IMAGES AND ALSO SHOW YOU PEOPLE WITH AN INTEREST THAT YOU CAN CONTACT TO GET FURTHER INFORMATION. YOU CAN ALSO LOOK UP LOCATIONS ON INSTAGRAM AND TWITTER TO SEE OTHER PEOPLE'S PHOTOS OF THAT AREA.

INTERVIEW PEOPLE

MOST PEOPLE WILL BE ONLY TOO HAPPY TO TELL YOU WHAT THEY KNOW ABOUT A CERTAIN JOB, AREA, EXPERIENCE ETC. BUT IN RETURN, ADD THEIR NAME TO THE THANK YOUS AT THE BEGINNING OF YOUR BOOK INCLUDING THEIR WEBSITE ETC. TO HELP THEM TOO! YOU CAN FIND THESE PEOPLE FROM YOUR KEYWORD SEARCH.

WATCH MOVIES THAT ARE SET IN THE AREA

GO ONTO AMAZON AND SEARCH FOR YOUR AREA OF RESEARCH AND THEN TYPE IN 'MOVIES/FILMS' ETC.

# RESEARCH

WHERE DO I GO FOR RESEARCH?

READ BOOKS SET IN THE TIME AND PLACE THAT YOU NEED TO RESEARCH

LOOK CLOSELY AT HOW THE AUTHOR DESCRIBES SOMETHING. DON'T COPY IT, OBVIOUSLY. BUT YOU WILL LEARN HOW TO ENHANCE YOUR OWN WRITING BY SEEING HOW SOMEBODY ELSE DESCRIBES THE SETTING/EXPERIENCE/JOB/FOOD ETC.

JOIN RELEVANT FACEBOOK GROUPS

THERE IS A FACEBOOK GROUP FOR EVERYTHING! GO TO THE SEARCH BAR ON FACEBOOK AND TYPE IN A KEYWORD SUCH AS 'TUDORS' (IF YOU'RE RESEARCHING HISTORY) OR 'FORMULA 1 CARS' FOR EXAMPLE.

HIRE A CONSULTANT

THIS IS LIKELY TO COST. GOOGLE SOMEBODY WHO SPECIALISES IN THE AREA YOU NEED. CHECK THEM OUT PROPERLY. SEE WHAT THEY HAVE DONE BEFORE.

RESEARCH

WHERE DO I GO FOR RESEARCH?

LIBRARY
Speak to the librarians for specialist subjects and where to go to get more information.

LAND REGISTRY
Use these to find old town plans and street layouts from yesteryear. Especially useful if you're writing about London in the 1500's for example.

CENSUS
This is great for names, jobs etc.

MUSEUMS
Especially important if you are writing a military novel or one about historical families/the aristocracy.

TRAVEL
Go to the places you are writing about, if they exist that is. Film or take pictures of your walkaround, to use for reference later.

RESEARCH

WHERE DO I GO FOR RESEARCH?

GO ON SITES SUCH AS QUORA

TYPE IN YOUR SEARCH TERM/KEYWORD. IF YOU LOOK UNDER 'QUESTIONS' YOU WILL SEE ALL THE QUESTIONS PEOPLE HAVE ASKED RELATING TO THAT SUBJECT AND LIKELY TO SEE MANY ANSWERS. THIS CAN BE A GREAT RESOURCE TOO.

USE SITES SUCH AS TRIPADVISOR

SEE HOW OTHERS DESCRIBE TOUR LOCATION, HOW THEY FEEL ABOUT IT AND ANY PICTURES THEY HAVE UPLOADED.

YOUTUBE VIDEOS

YOUTUBE IS A SEARCH ENGINE TOO. TYPE IN EXACTLY WHAT YOU ARE LOOKING FOR.

 # RESEARCH

WHAT TO DO NOW?

FILL IN THE BLANKS BELOW OF THE DIFFERENT PLACES YOU WILL GO TO RESEARCH FOR THAT PARTICULAR QUESTION.

EG. I NEED TO FIND OUT A DOCTOR'S WORKING CONDITIONS.

WHERE TO GO?

SEARCH FOR A DOCTOR ON TWITTER UNDER 'PEOPLE' AND LOOK FOR ONE THAT LOOKS LEGITIMATE. ONE WAY TO TELL THIS IS TO LOOK FOR THE 'BLUE TICK' BY THEIR NAME. THIS MEANS THEY ARE VERIFIED AS BEING WHO THEY SAY THEY ARE.

YOU CAN ASK IF YOU CAN SEND THEM A DM (DIRECT MESSAGE) AND IF THEY GIVE YOU PERMISSION THEN SEND YOUR REQUEST. MAKE SURE YOU SAY SOMETHING LIKE, 'I WILL BE SURE TO ADD YOUR NAME TO MY LIST OF THANK YOUS AT THE BEGINNING OF THE BOOK AND IF YOU WOULD LIKE A WEBSITE ETC. PROMOTING THEN I'D BE HAPPY TO DO SO.' OR WORDS TO THAT EFFECT.

RESEARCH

GO OVER ALL THE NOTES YOU HAVE SO FAR, ESPECIALLY THE FULL CHARACTER DESCRIPTIONS.

WRITE IN THE SPACES BELOW ALL OF THE THINGS YOU NEED TO RESEARCH.

IF THERE'S SOMETHING BY WHICH YOU HAVE WRITTEN 'NEED TO KNOW MORE ABOUT THAT PLACE/FOOD/HOBBY/JOB ETC...' THEN IT GETS RESEARCHED TO MAKE IT MORE AUTHENTIC IN YOUR STORY.

BELOW IS SOME SPACE TO RECORD YOUR RESEARCH NEEDED. LEAVE THE 'WHERE SHOULD I LOOK' BLANK FOR NOW.

1..

WHERE SHOULD I LOOK?
....

2..

WHERE SHOULD I LOOK?
....

3..

WHERE SHOULD I LOOK?
....

RESEARCH

4. ....

WHERE SHOULD I LOOK?
....

5. ....

WHERE SHOULD I LOOK?
....

6. ....

WHERE SHOULD I LOOK?
....

7. ....

WHERE SHOULD I LOOK?
....

8. ....

WHERE SHOULD I LOOK?
....

9. ....

WHERE SHOULD I LOOK?
....

RESEARCH

10 ....

WHERE SHOULD I LOOK?
....

11 ....

WHERE SHOULD I LOOK?
....

12 ....

WHERE SHOULD I LOOK?
....

13 ....

WHERE SHOULD I LOOK?
....

14 ....

WHERE SHOULD I LOOK?
....

15 ....

WHERE SHOULD I LOOK?
....

RESEARCH

16. ....

WHERE SHOULD I LOOK?
....

17. ....

WHERE SHOULD I LOOK?
....

18. ....

WHERE SHOULD I LOOK?
....

19. ....

WHERE SHOULD I LOOK?
....

20. ....

WHERE SHOULD I LOOK?
....

21. ....

WHERE SHOULD I LOOK?
....

LOCATIONS

WHAT TO DO

THINK OF YOUR MAIN 3 LOCATIONS.

FILL IN THE BLANKS AFTER DOING YOUR RESEARCH SO THAT YOU CAN COME BACK TO IT WHEN YOU ARE WRITING.

LOCATIONS

LOCATION 1: ....

- WHAT TYPE OF PEOPLE LIVE THERE/LIVE NEAR BY/WORK THERE?

- WHAT IS THE LANDSCAPE LIKE?

- ARE THE LOCALS FRIENDLY/CAUTIOUS/SUSPICIOUS/HAPPY? WHY?

- WHAT DOES A NORMAL DAY LOOK LIKE IN THIS LOCATION? WHAT CAN YOU SEE/HEAR/SMELL?

LOCATIONS

LOCATION 1: ....

- WHAT WOULD THE COMPLETE OPPOSITE LOOK LIKE? WHY?

- DOES IT GET MANY VISITORS?

- WHAT IS IT KNOWN FOR?

# LOCATIONS

LOCATION 2: ....

- WHAT TYPE OF PEOPLE LIVE THERE/LIVE NEAR BY/WORK THERE?

- WHAT IS THE LANDSCAPE LIKE?

- ARE THE LOCALS FRIENDLY/CAUTIOUS/SUSPICIOUS/HAPPY? WHY?

- WHAT DOES A NORMAL DAY LOOK LIKE IN THIS LOCATION? WHAT CAN YOU SEE/HEAR/SMELL?

LOCATIONS

LOCATION 2: ....

- WHAT WOULD THE COMPLETE OPPOSITE LOOK LIKE? WHY?

- DOES IT GET MANY VISITORS?

- WHAT IS IT KNOWN FOR?

LOCATIONS

LOCATION 3: ....

- WHAT TYPE OF PEOPLE LIVE THERE/LIVE NEAR BY/WORK THERE?

- WHAT IS THE LANDSCAPE LIKE?

- ARE THE LOCALS FRIENDLY/CAUTIOUS/SUSPICIOUS/HAPPY? WHY?

- WHAT DOES A NORMAL DAY LOOK LIKE IN THIS LOCATION? WHAT CAN YOU SEE/HEAR/SMELL?

# LOCATIONS

LOCATION 3: ....

- WHAT WOULD THE COMPLETE OPPOSITE LOOK LIKE? WHY?

- DOES IT GET MANY VISITORS?

- WHAT IS IT KNOWN FOR?

PLOT TWIST IDEAS:

MAKE YOUR READERS GO "WOW!"

WHAT NOT TO DO!

- DON'T MAKE IT TOO OBVIOUS! THIS IS A CLICHE. NEVER EVER USE "IT WAS ALL A DREAM" IN YOUR STORY AT ANY TIME! REMEMBER, READERS HAVE INVESTED IN YOUR STORY. THIS WILL COME ACROSS AS LAZY AND THEY WILL BE HIGHLY ANNOYED!

- MAKE IT UNBELIEVABLE! OTHERWISE, READERS WILL SWITCH OFF. YOU CAN MAKE YOUR PLOT TWISTS MASSIVE. AS LONG AS YOU HAVE PUT IN THE STEPS BEFOREHAND YOUR READERS WILL BELIEVE YOUR PLOT TWIST.

IDEAS

- KILL OFF A CHARACTER THAT SHOULDN'T BE KILLED OFF - MAKE YOUR READER GO, "NOOOO!!! THEY CAN'T DIE!! WHAT'S GOING TO HAPPEN NOW?"

- MAKE A CHARACTER BE RELATED TO ANOTHER CHARACTER - ONE THEY DIDN'T KNOW ABOUT. THINK STAR WARS AND DARTH VADER/LUKE SKYWALKER. WHAT'S THE REASON FOR THE SECRECY? THIS COULD EVEN BE AN IDEA FOR ANOTHER STORY IN THE FUTURE.

- THE MAIN CHARACTER WAS ACTUALLY THE VILLAIN ALL ALONG! - WHY?

- THERE'S AN EVEN BIGGER PROBLEM TO SOLVE WHEN YOU THINK YOU'VE REACHED 'THE END' - THIS MAKES YOUR READER GO, "WHOA!" THEY THINK IT'S ALL SAFE BUT THERE IS ONE LAST TASK AND IT'S MASSIVE AND TOTALLY UNEXPECTED.

- THE 'DEAD' ARE NOT REALLY DEAD - BRING BACK A VILLAIN WHO ISN'T ACTUALLY DEAD RIGHT AT THE TIME IT ALL SEEMS SAFE.

PLOT TWIST IDEAS:
MAKE YOUR READERS GO "WOW!"

IDEAS

- THE 'BAD GUYS' BECOME 'GOOD' - WHY WOULD THIS HAPPEN? WHEN? THE BEST TIME IS WHEN THE READER THINKS IT IS CERTAIN DEATH FOR THE MAIN CHARACTER AT THE HANDS OF THIS 'BAD GUY.'

- THE 'GOOD GUY' IS THE 'BAD GUY' ALL ALONG - WHY WOULD THEY HAVE TO KEEP THEIR IDENTITY A SECRET? WHAT DO THEY GAIN?

- YOUR MAIN CHARACTER FALLS ILL RIGHT AT THE 'WRONG' TIME - WHAT WILL HAPPEN TO THEM? THIS WOULD WORK WELL JUST AFTER A VICTORY OR RIGHT BEFORE SOMETHING IMPORTANT. WHAT COULD THAT BE?

- SOMEBODY 'STUPID' WAS 'RIGHT ALL ALONG' - WHY DIDN'T PEOPLE BELIEVE THEM? WHAT ARE THE CONSEQUENCES OF THIS?

- SOMEBODY 'STUPID' WAS THE 'VILLAIN ALL ALONG' - WHAT WAS THEIR MOTIVE?

- THERE WAS A MISTAKEN IDENTITY ALL ALONG - WHAT IF SOMEBODY HAS BEEN FOLLOWED/KILLED AND THEY WEREN'T THE INTENDED PERSON? WHAT ARE THE CONSEQUENCES?

- YOUR MAIN CHARACTER WRECKS THE DESIRED OUTCOME BY MISTAKE - WHAT HAPPENS NOW?

- YOUR MAIN CHARACTER FREEZES AT THE POINT OF ACTION - WHY? NOW, WHAT HAPPENS?

PLOT TWIST IDEAS:

MAKE YOUR READERS GO "WOW!"

NOW WHAT?

- PICK 2-3 PLOT TWISTS YOU LIKE THE SOUND OF (OR OTHERS IF YOU HAVE IDEAS).

- THINK 'HOW CAN I APPLY THIS PLOT TWIST TO EACH OF MY STORIES?' AND GO THROUGH ALL OF YOUR CHARACTERS. SOMETHING WILL SPARK - AND THAT'S YOUR PLOT TWIST.

- THINK OF THE 5-STEPS TO MAKING IT BELIEVABLE. THESE ARE GOING TO BE VERY SUBTLE HINTS/CONVERSATIONS/SCENES THAT LEAD UP TO THE PLOT TWIST. WRITE EACH THING SEPARATELY ON AN INDEX CARD.

PLOT TWIST IDEAS:
MAKE YOUR READERS GO "WOW!"

PLOT TWIST IDEAS I THINK WOULD BE EXCITING FOR MY STORY - GO THROUGH THE LIST ABOVE:
1. ....
....

WOULD MY READER EVER IMAGINE THIS HAPPENING? IF YES, TWEAK IT!!
....
....

HOW WOULD THIS PLOT TWIST CHANGE THE DYNAMICS OF THE STORY?
....
....

WHAT 5 STEPS (AT LEAST) WOULD I HAVE TO INCLUDE BEFOREHAND TO ENSURE THE 'REVEAL' (THE PLOT TWIST) IS BELIEVABLE?
1. ....
2. ....
3. ....
4. ....
5. ....

WHEREABOUTS IN THE STORY CAN I SEE THIS PLOT TWIST HAPPENING?
ACT 1 ....
ACT 2 ....
ACT 3 ....

NOTES:
....
....

PLOT TWIST IDEAS:

MAKE YOUR READERS GO "WOW!"

PLOT TWIST IDEAS I THINK WOULD BE EXCITING FOR MY STORY - GO THROUGH THE LIST ABOVE:

2..
....

WOULD MY READER EVER IMAGINE THIS HAPPENING? IF YES, TWEAK IT!!
....
....

HOW WOULD THIS PLOT TWIST CHANGE THE DYNAMICS OF THE STORY?
....
....

WHAT 5 STEPS (AT LEAST) WOULD I HAVE TO INCLUDE BEFOREHAND TO ENSURE THE 'REVEAL' (THE PLOT TWIST) IS BELIEVABLE?

1..
2..
3..
4..
5..

WHEREABOUTS IN THE STORY CAN I SEE THIS PLOT TWIST HAPPENING?

ACT 1..
ACT 2..
ACT 3..

NOTES:
....
....

PLOT TWIST IDEAS:
MAKE YOUR READERS GO "WOW!"

PLOT TWIST IDEAS I THINK WOULD BE EXCITING FOR MY STORY - GO THROUGH THE LIST ABOVE:

3...
....

WOULD MY READER EVER IMAGINE THIS HAPPENING? IF YES, TWEAK IT!!
....
....

HOW WOULD THIS PLOT TWIST CHANGE THE DYNAMICS OF THE STORY?
....
....

WHAT 5 STEPS (AT LEAST) WOULD I HAVE TO INCLUDE BEFOREHAND TO ENSURE THE 'REVEAL' (THE PLOT TWIST) IS BELIEVABLE?

1...
2...
3...
4...
5...

WHEREABOUTS IN THE STORY CAN I SEE THIS PLOT TWIST HAPPENING?

ACT 1...
ACT 2...
ACT 3...

NOTES:
....
....

THE WALLOP SCENE – AN EXPLANATION

WHAT IS A WALLOP SCENE?

A 'WALLOP SCENE' IS A SCENE THAT GETS THE READER STUCK IN STRAIGHT AWAY. IT CAN BE THE VERY FIRST SCENE OR IF NOT, ONE OF THE EARLIEST SCENES.

FOR EXAMPLE:

EVER WATCH A CRIME DRAMA? THE VERY FIRST SCENE MAY BE QUITE CALM THEN ALL OF A SUDDEN SOMEBODY GETS SHOT. THERE'S HARDLY ANY DIALOGUE AND IT LEAVES YOU THINKING 'WOW! WHAT JUST HAPPENED?' THEN IT GOES TO A DIFFERENT SCENE THAT IS CALM AGAIN.

THE WALLOP SCENE 'WAKES YOU UP' AND IMMEDIATELY MAKES YOU ASK QUESTIONS AND SETS THE TONE.

YOU DON'T HAVE TO BE WRITING CRIME TO MAKE THIS WORK.

YOU COULD BE WRITING A ROM-COM AND SOMETHING COMPLETELY HUMILIATING COULD HAPPEN TO YOUR MAIN CHARACTER, SEEMINGLY OUT OF THE BLUE, BUT IT GIVES YOU A TASTE OF THINGS TO COME WITH THE BOOK OR WITH THAT CHARACTER.

THE WALLOP SCENE – AN EXPLANATION

WHAT COULD YOUR WALLOP SCENE BE?

Think of your storyline and your characters. You know them pretty well now. What could be a scene with the main character/s where the reader can 'see' exactly what they are like, how they would act, or a struggle they have – but in a big way?

FOR EXAMPLE:

Somebody who is painfully shy, at the very beginning of the book may be waiting to go out on stage. They get introduced, they walk out on stage, their big moment arrives (and by this point, the reader has no clue) the character is about to open their mouth and... nothing. Complete humiliation.

They then run off stage to boos and confusion.

Can you see it gets the reader involved straight away rather than explaining that the main character is shy? Let's humiliate them instead!

THE WALLOP SCENE - AN EXPLANATION

WHAT COULD YOUR WALLOP SCENE BE?

OR...

YOU COULD HAVE A BRIDE WALKING DOWN THE AISLE LOOKING RADIANT. HER EYES MEET HER HUSBAND-TO-BE'S, THEY ARE ABOUT TO SAY 'I DO' WHEN HE SAYS..... 'I DON'T LOVE YOU ANYMORE' AND LEAVES THE CHURCH WHERE EVERYBODY IS LEFT OPEN-MOUTHED.

WHAT A START TO A STORY! WHAT THE HELL IS THE BRIDE GOING TO DO NOW? HOW WILL THIS AFFECT HER?

WALLOP SCENES ARE DESIGNED TO DUMP YOUR READER HEAD-FIRST INTO A CONFLICT, STRUGGLE OR SITUATION. WHERE THEY CAN'T HELP BUT BE HOOKED AND WANT TO READ ON.

LET'S MAKE IT A GOOD ONE!

THE WALLOP SCENE

WHAT DO I DO NOW?

THINK OF 3 WALLOP SCENES. ROTATE YOUR MAIN CHARACTERS. CHOOSE THE BIGGEST WALLOP THAT SHOWS OFF THEIR CHARACTERISTICS. MAKE SURE THIS IS HOW YOU WANT THEM TO ACT IN ACT 1!

IDEA 1

WALLOP FACTOR (OUT OF 10) ....

IDEA 2

WALLOP FACTOR (OUT OF 10) ....

IDEA 3

WALLOP FACTOR (OUT OF 10) ....

THE BASICS

TITLE: ....

WHO IS THE MAIN CHARACTER? (BRIEF DESCRIPTION)

WHO IS AN ALLY? WHY? WHAT COULD THEY LOSE/GAIN? WHY?

WHAT IS THE MAIN CHARACTER'S EXTERNAL GOAL?

THE BASICS

WHO IS THE MAIN ANTAGONIST? (BRIEF DESCRIPTION)

ROUGH ENDING?

THE BASIC PLAN

BOOK TITLE..
MAIN CHARACTER'S NAME..

ACT 1:

WHAT IS THE CHARACTER'S PROBLEM/ISSUE? (EXTERNAL MOTIVATION)

WHAT LESSON DO THEY NEED TO LEARN? (INTERNAL MOTIVATION)

WHAT IS THEIR 'WHY'?

WHO IS THEIR GUIDE TO HELP THEM?

WHAT'S THE PLAN?

THE BASIC PLAN

BOOK TITLE...

MAIN CHARACTER'S NAME..

ACT 2:

WHAT INPUT DOES THE GUIDE HAVE WITH THE PLAN AND WHAT DANGERS DO THEY BOTH FACE?

THE BASIC PLAN

BOOK TITLE..
MAIN CHARACTER'S NAME...

ACT 3:

WHAT DOES THE PLAN LOOK LIKE IF IT IS A SUCCESS?

WHAT DOES IT LOOK LIKE IF IT IS A FAILURE?

YOUR OPENING LINE

HAVE AN IDEA ABOUT THE SCENE FIRST:

- LOCATION/SETTING?

- WEATHER?

- WHAT IS THE FIRST SCENE?

- TIME OF DAY?

YOUR OPENING LINE

- PICK 3-4 POWER WORDS YOU LIKED FROM THE GENRE BUNDLE.

- WRITE 2-3 VERBS THAT APPEAL TO YOU AND ARE RELATED TO YOUR STORY.

  EXAMPLES: RAN, ACCUSED, AIMED, APPROACHED, ASKED, AVOID, BELIEVED, BREAK, BURST, COULD, CLIMBED, COMMITTED, DARED, DEMANDED, DESIRED, DESTROYED, DOUBTED, DREAMED, ENTERED, EXPLAINED, FEEL, FINISHED, FOLLOWED, FORGET, HESITATED, HOPED, IMAGINED, INTENDED, INVESTIGATE, JUMPED, KEPT, KISSED, LAUGHED, LEARNED, LIED, LOOKED, LOVED, MISSED, NEGLECTED, OWED, PAY, PLAYED, PREPARED, REALISE, REGRET, SETTLE, SHUT, STEAL, TALK, TOLERATE, WISH, UNDERSTAND, PROMISE, APPEARED.

VERB 1:

VERB 2:

VERB 3:

- WHAT EMOTION DO YOU WANT TO ACHIEVE IN THIS SCENE?

YOUR OPENING LINE

- NOW FREE WRITE YOUR FIRST PARAGRAPH USING THE INFORMATION FROM THE ABOVE. DO NOT EDIT!

- RE-READ THE PARAGRAPH ABOVE. CIRCLE OR UNDERLINE THE SECOND YOU FEEL IT GETS TO THE ACTION.

- THIS IS YOUR FIRST LINE!

MY FIRST LINE IS:

THE 'ALMOST FINAL' PLAN

WHAT TO DO

FILL IN THE BLANKS.

WE ARE PUTTING IT TOGETHER.

THIS IS GETTING TO THE EXCITING BIT.

NOW IS THE TIME TO PUT IN ANY IDEAS/SCENES YOU WANT TO INCLUDE IN THE SPACES PROVIDED.

THE 'ALMOST FINAL' PLAN

- BOOK TITLE AND NUMBER? (IF PART OF A SERIES):

  TITLE:

  NUMBER:

- SCENE I REALLY WANT TO INCLUDE?

- WHY IS THE SCENE RELEVANT?

- WHERE IN THE STORY SHOULD THIS SCENE GO? CIRCLE

ACT 1	BEGINNING	MIDDLE	END
ACT 2	BEGINNING	MIDDLE	END
ACT 3	BEGINNING	MIDDLE	END

THE 'ALMOST FINAL' PLAN

- SCENE I REALLY WANT TO INCLUDE?

- WHY IS THE SCENE RELEVANT?

- WHERE IN THE STORY SHOULD THIS SCENE GO? CIRCLE

ACT 1	BEGINNING	MIDDLE	END
ACT 2	BEGINNING	MIDDLE	END
ACT 3	BEGINNING	MIDDLE	END

THE 'ALMOST FINAL' PLAN

- SCENE I REALLY WANT TO INCLUDE?

- WHY IS THE SCENE RELEVANT?

- WHERE IN THE STORY SHOULD THIS SCENE GO? CIRCLE

ACT 1	BEGINNING	MIDDLE	END
ACT 2	BEGINNING	MIDDLE	END
ACT 3	BEGINNING	MIDDLE	END

THE 'ALMOST FINAL' PLAN

ACT 1

- WHICH CHARACTERS APPEAR IN ACT 1?

NAME:

HOW WILL THEY ACT?

NAME:

HOW WILL THEY ACT?

NAME:

HOW WILL THEY ACT?

NAME:

HOW WILL THEY ACT?

THE 'ALMOST FINAL' PLAN

ACT 1

- WHICH CHARACTERS APPEAR IN ACT 1?

NAME:

HOW WILL THEY ACT?

NAME:

HOW WILL THEY ACT?

NAME:

HOW WILL THEY ACT?

NAME:

HOW WILL THEY ACT?

THE 'ALMOST FINAL' PLAN

ACT 1

- INCITING EVENTS - MAKE THEM BIG!

IDEA 1:

IDEA 2:

IDEA 3:

- PICK WHICH INCITING EVENT HAS THE BIGGEST WOW!

MOST EFFECTIVE INCITING EVENT:

THE 'ALMOST FINAL' PLAN

ACT 1

- WHAT NEEDS TO HAPPEN IN ACT 1?

- LOCATIONS IN ACT 1?

THE 'ALMOST FINAL' PLAN

ACT 2

RED HERRING IDEAS:

• WHICH CHARACTERS APPEAR IN ACT 2?

NAME:

HOW WILL THEY ACT?

NAME:

HOW WILL THEY ACT?

NAME:

HOW WILL THEY ACT?

NAME:

HOW WILL THEY ACT?

THE 'ALMOST FINAL' PLAN

ACT 2

RED HERRING IDEAS:

• WHICH CHARACTERS APPEAR IN ACT 2?

NAME:

HOW WILL THEY ACT?

NAME:

HOW WILL THEY ACT?

NAME:

HOW WILL THEY ACT?

NAME:

HOW WILL THEY ACT?

THE 'ALMOST FINAL' PLAN

ACT 2

- WHAT NEEDS TO HAPPEN IN ACT 2?

- LOCATIONS IN ACT 2?

THE 'ALMOST FINAL' PLAN

ACT 2

- PLOT TWISTS - MAKE THEM EXCITING!

IDEA 1:

IDEA 2:

IDEA 3:

- PICK WHICH PLOT TWIST HAS THE BIGGEST WOW!

MOST EFFECTIVE PLOT TWIST:

THE 'ALMOST FINAL' PLAN

ACT 3

- WHICH CHARACTERS APPEAR IN ACT 3?

NAME:

HOW WILL THEY ACT?

NAME:

HOW WILL THEY ACT?

NAME:

HOW WILL THEY ACT?

NAME:

HOW WILL THEY ACT?

THE 'ALMOST FINAL' PLAN

ACT 3

- WHICH CHARACTERS APPEAR IN ACT 3?

NAME:

HOW WILL THEY ACT?

NAME:

HOW WILL THEY ACT?

NAME:

HOW WILL THEY ACT?

NAME:

HOW WILL THEY ACT?

THE 'ALMOST FINAL' PLAN

ACT 3

- WHAT NEEDS TO HAPPEN IN ACT 3?

- LOCATIONS IN ACT 3?

THE 'ALMOST FINAL' PLAN

ACT 3

- IDEAS FOR GREAT ENDINGS - MAKE THEM EXCITING!

IDEA 1:

IDEA 2:

IDEA 3:

- PICK WHICH ENDING IDEA HAS THE BIGGEST WOW!

MOST EFFECTIVE ENDING IDEA:

THE COMPLETE PLAN FOR WRITING YOUR BOOK

TITLE ....

1. OPENING LINE - MAKE IT ACTIVE. DIALOGUE WORKS WELL.

2. OPENING SCENE (THE WALLOP). MAKE IT A WOW, REMEMBER! SHOW NOT TELL THE SETTING, AND USE THE 5 SENSES.

3. FIRST LOOK AT YOUR CHARACTERS 'NORMAL' LIFE - WHAT ARE THEY DOING? DESCRIBE THEIR BASIC ROUTINE.
REMEMBER, SHOW NOT TELL. SET THE MOOD AND THE TONE HERE. SHOW A FLAW OR TWO OF YOUR MAIN CHARACTER AND HOW IT'S AFFECTING THEM. DESCRIBE THE SETTING. USE INFORMATION FROM ALL YOUR NOTES. WHAT TRAITS ARE THEY SHOWING? REMEMBER SETTING AND SENSES.

THE COMPLETE PLAN FOR WRITING YOUR BOOK

WHAT LESSON DOES THE MAIN CHARACTER NEED TO LEARN AND WHY? WHAT HAPPENS IF THEY DON'T? WHO TELLS THEM THEY NEED TO LEARN THIS AND WHY? HOW HAVE THEY ARRIVED AT THIS?

THIS COULD BE A SENTENCE OR A SCENE. DON'T FORGET A DESCRIPTION OF THE SETTING AND TO USE THE 5 SENSES.

4. WHAT DOES THE MAIN CHARACTER WANT AND WHY? WHAT ARE THEIR MOTIVATIONS AND GOALS AND WHY DO THEY THINK IT WILL FIX THEIR LIFE? THIS COULD BE A SITUATION THEY ARE IN OR A CONVERSATION. SHOW DON'T TELL. REMEMBER THE 5 SENSES. WHAT TRAITS ARE THEY SHOWING?

THE COMPLETE PLAN FOR WRITING YOUR BOOK

5. MENTION SOME MORE FLAWS OF THE MAIN CHARACTER AND HOW THIS AFFECTS THEIR DAILY LIFE AND WHOM IT IMPACTS AND WHY?
SHOW DON'T TELL.

6. THE INCITING EVENT (CATALYST) AND WHY? WHAT IS THE IMPACT ON EVERYBODY AROUND THEM AND WHY? THIS COULD BE A LIFE-CHANGING EVENT, BAD NEWS ETC. IT'S A WAKE-UP CALL OR CALL TO ACTION. MAKE IT SO YOUR READERS SAY 'I DIDN'T SEE THAT COMING!' AND 'HOW ARE THEY GOING TO RECOVER FROM THAT?' MAKE IT BIG! PICK YOUR VERY BEST IDEA FROM PREVIOUS NOTES. WHAT ARE THE EMOTIONS OF THIS SCENE?
WHAT DO YOU WANT THE READER TO FEEL? WHAT TRAITS ARE THEY SHOWING?
WHAT COULD THE ANTAGONIST BE THINKING/DOING/FEELING? SHOW DON'T TELL.

THE COMPLETE PLAN FOR WRITING YOUR BOOK

7. THE REACTION TO THE INCITING EVENT - NOT VERY LONG, BUT THE CHARACTER/S CONSIDER WHAT WILL HAPPEN, WHO WILL BE IMPACTED AND WHY? THE CHARACTER WILL DECIDE HOW THEY WILL PROCEED. SHOW THE STRUGGLE AND CONVERSATIONS INVOLVED. REMEMBER SETTING AND SENSES.

8. WHEN/HOW/WHY DOES THE CHARACTER REALISE THEIR EXTERNAL GOAL? WHAT HAPPENS IF/WHEN THEY GET IT? WHAT TRAITS ARE THEY SHOWING DURING CONVERSATIONS OR INTERACTIONS DURING THIS TIME? WHAT COULD THE ANTAGONIST BE THINKING/DOING/FEELING? SHOW DON'T TELL.

THE COMPLETE PLAN FOR WRITING YOUR BOOK

9. WHEN/HOW/WHY CHARACTER REALISES THE EXTERNAL GOAL. WHAT HAPPENS IF THEY DON'T GET IT? CONVERSATION OR SCENE. REMEMBER SETTING AND 5 SENSES. WHAT TRAITS ARE THEY SHOWING?

10. WHAT CHARACTER FLAW WILL HINDER THE CHARACTER FROM ACHIEVING THIS EXTERNAL GOAL AND WHY? WHAT IS THE IMPACT AND WHY? WHERE IS THE CHARACTER GOING? WHERE ARE THEY? WHOM ARE THEY TALKING TO? WHAT COULD THE ANTAGONIST BE THINKING/DOING/FEELING? SHOW DON'T TELL THIS.

THE COMPLETE PLAN FOR WRITING YOUR BOOK

11. WHAT IS THEIR DRIVE FOR THEIR GOAL AND WHY? INTERNAL DIALOGUE, FEARS ETC. WHOM DO THEY TALK TO AND WHY? SETTING AND SENSES. WHAT IS THE "WORRY?" WHAT DO THEY SAY IS THE WORST THING TO HAPPEN?

WHAT COULD THE ANTAGONIST BE THINKING/DOING/FEELING? SHOW DON'T TELL THIS.

WHAT WILL THE READER BE THINKING AND WHY?

THE COMPLETE PLAN FOR WRITING YOUR BOOK

ACT TWO

12. THWART NO.1 TO THE GOAL. MAKE THIS A BIG ONE. WHAT WOULD HAVE TO HAPPEN TO REALLY UPSET THAT CHARACTER? WHAT IS THE CHARACTER'S ACHILLES HEEL?

WHAT WENT WRONG? BY WHO AND WHY?

WHAT DOES THE CHARACTER/S FEEL?

REMEMBER SETTING AND SENSES. HOW DO THEY FIND OUT ABOUT THE THING GOING WRONG? WHAT TRAITS ARE THEY SHOWING?

THE COMPLETE PLAN FOR WRITING YOUR BOOK

13. PLOT TWIST - MAKE IT BIG! MAKE IT UNPREDICTABLE.

WHAT ARE THE EMOTIONS OF THIS SCENE? WHAT DO YOU WANT THE READER TO FEEL? REMEMBER SETTING AND SENSES.

WHAT WOULD BE SOMETHING THAT YOUR MAIN CHARACTER WOULD HATE TO HAPPEN AND WHY?

14. CHARACTERS NEW DRIVE FOR THEIR GOAL AND WHY? WHO IS NOW HELPING THEM AND WHY? INTRODUCE A NEW CHARACTER ALLY. WHAT CONVERSATIONS ARE TAKING PLACE? REMEMBER SETTING AND SENSES. WHAT ARE THEY DOING AND WHY?

THE COMPLETE PLAN FOR WRITING YOUR BOOK

15. TIME TO ADD IN A RED HERRING. WHO/WHAT IS THIS? HAVE A COUPLE TO CHOOSE FROM THEN CHOOSE YOUR FAVOURITE. START TO LEAD YOUR READERS DOWN THE WRONG ROUTE.

16. HOW'S THE NEW PLAN GOING? PROBABLY GOING WRONG. EVEN A DEAD END. WHY? WHAT ARE THE CHARACTERS INVOLVED SAYING AND WHY? WHERE ARE THESE CONVERSATIONS TAKING PLACE? REMEMBER SETTING AND SENSES. WHAT ARE THE TRAITS OF THE CHARACTERS INVOLVED AT THIS POINT?

THE COMPLETE PLAN FOR WRITING YOUR BOOK

17. ANTAGONIST ATTACKS! WHO IS THIS? WHY? WHEN AND HOW? WHERE DID THIS TAKE PLACE? REMEMBER SETTING AND SENSES.

WHAT CONVERSATIONS/ACTIONS ARE TAKING PLACE?

WHAT ARE THE EMOTIONS OF THIS SCENE?

WHAT DO YOU WANT THE READER TO FEEL?

THE COMPLETE PLAN FOR WRITING YOUR BOOK

18. CHARACTER'S NEW DRIVE FOR GOAL. WHO/WHY/WHEN/WHERE? WHO IS HELPING THEM AND WHY? WHERE ARE THESE CONVERSATIONS TAKING PLACE? REMEMBER SETTING AND SENSES.

WHAT ARE THE EMOTIONS OF THIS SCENE? WHAT DO YOU WANT THE READER TO FEEL? WHAT ARE THE CONSEQUENCES OF THIS NEW DRIVE/PLAN GOING WRONG?

WHAT IS AT STAKE? WHY?

WHAT COULD THE ANTAGONIST BE THINKING/DOING/FEELING? SHOW DON'T TELL THIS.

# THE COMPLETE PLAN FOR WRITING YOUR BOOK

19. THE BIG COUNTDOWN. THE URGENCY. WHAT HAPPENS IF THE CLOCK TICKS DOWN TO ZERO? IMPACT? ON WHO? WHY?

HAVE A CHARACTER SAY SOMETHING LIKE 'IMAGINE IF...' HAVE THEM THEN SPEAK THEIR WORRIES ABOUT THE CONSEQUENCES.

WHAT COULD THE ANTAGONIST BE THINKING/DOING/FEELING? SHOW DON'T TELL THIS.

THE COMPLETE PLAN FOR WRITING YOUR BOOK

21. FALSE VICTORY CELEBRATION. BY WHO? WHY? WHEN? WHERE? WHOM DID IT IMPACT? WHY? AT A PARTY/GATHERING?

REMEMBER SETTING AND SENSES.

WHAT COULD THE ANTAGONIST BE THINKING/DOING/FEELING? SHOW DON'T TELL THIS.

THE COMPLETE PLAN FOR WRITING YOUR BOOK

22. PLOT TWIST - MAKE IT TOTALLY UNPREDICTABLE. USE YOUR NOTES, UNLESS YOU HAVE HAD A NEW IDEA BY NOW. WHAT ARE THE EMOTIONS OF THIS SCENE? WHAT DO YOU WANT THE READER TO FEEL?

MAKE IT BIG! WHAT WOULD BE THE WORST THING TO HAPPEN AT THIS PARTICULAR TIME AND WHY?

REMEMBER SETTING AND SENSES

SHOW THE TRAITS OF THE CHARACTERS IN THIS TYPE OF SITUATION.

THE COMPLETE PLAN FOR WRITING YOUR BOOK

23. WHAT DOES THE MAIN CHARACTER NEED NOW AND WHY? WHAT HAPPENS IF THEY DON'T GET IT AND WHY?

WHAT CONVERSATIONS ARE TAKING PLACE AND WITH WHO?

DOES ANYBODY DISAGREE WITH THEM?

WHAT ARE THE EMOTIONS OF THIS SCENE?

WHAT DO YOU WANT THE READER TO FEEL OR SAY OUT LOUD?

THE COMPLETE PLAN FOR WRITING YOUR BOOK

24. ANTAGONIST ATTACKS AGAIN AND THE BAD GUYS CLOSE IN. THE CLOCK IS TICKING DOWN.

EXACTLY WHAT HAPPENS. HOW IS THE PRESSURE CRANKED UP? WHO DOES THIS IMPACT AND WHY?

THE SITUATION GOES FROM BAD TO WORSE. WHAT DO THE CHARACTERS FEEL DURING THIS TIME AND WHY?

REMEMBER SETTING AND SENSES!

WHAT ARE THE EMOTIONS OF THIS SCENE? WHAT DO YOU WANT THE READER TO FEEL? WHAT CONVERSATIONS ARE TAKING PLACE AND BY WHOM?

HINT: WHAT WOULD BE THE WORST THING TO HAPPEN TO YOUR MAIN CHARACTER OR ALLY DURING THIS TIME? USE YOUR NOTES. WHAT IS YOUR CHARACTER'S ACHILLES HEEL?

THE COMPLETE PLAN FOR WRITING YOUR BOOK

25. WHO COMES TO HELP? WHY? WHAT HAPPENS IF THEY DON'T AND WHY?

TALK ABOUT THE CONSEQUENCES. WHAT IS THE WORST THING TO HAPPEN AND WHY?

WHAT CONVERSATIONS ARE HAPPENING? DOES ANYBODY DISAGREE AND WHY? HAVE CHARACTERS HAVE A 'WHAT DO WE DO' CONVERSATION.

REMEMBER THE SETTING AND SENSES.

THE COMPLETE PLAN FOR WRITING YOUR BOOK

26. THE FIRST BATTLE SCENE - WHO IS INVOLVED AND WHY?

WHICH CHARACTERS ARE AFFECTED BY THE OUTCOME?

WHAT IS THE IMPACT ON ALL THE OTHER CHARACTERS? ARE THERE ANY CASUALTIES (METAPHORICALLY AND PHYSICALLY)?

WHAT EMOTIONAL IMPACT IS THERE?

THE COMPLETE PLAN FOR WRITING YOUR BOOK

27. IT'S ALL GONE BADLY WRONG! IT IS YOUR MAIN CHARACTER'S FAULT. HOW DO THEY FEEL? WHY? WHICH TRAITS ARE THEY EXHIBITING?

REMEMBER SHOW NOT TELL.

WHAT COULD ANOTHER 'WORST THING TO HAPPEN' BE? WHAT ARE THE CONVERSATIONS TAKING PLACE?

REMEMBER SETTING AND SENSES.

WHAT EMOTION DO YOU WANT YOUR READERS TO FEEL?

WHAT COULD THE ANTAGONIST BE THINKING/FEELING/DOING? SHOW DON'T TELL.

THE COMPLETE PLAN FOR WRITING YOUR BOOK

28. WHAT HAPPENS NOW? WHAT MUST YOUR CHARACTERS DO AND WHY? DO THEY HAVE TO 'DIG DEEP'?

WHAT INNER DEMONS/CONFLICTS DO THEY HAVE TO WRESTLE WITH AND WHY?

WHAT IS THE IMPACT OF THIS ON THE OTHER CHARACTERS? WHY? WHAT IS THEIR REACTION?

HOW IS/ARE THE MAIN CHARACTER(S) FEELING? WHAT TRAITS ARE THEY SHOWING?

REMEMBER SHOW NOT TELL.

THE COMPLETE PLAN FOR WRITING YOUR BOOK

ACT THREE

29. HOW WILL THE CHARACTER FIX THINGS THE RIGHT WAY?

WHAT HAVE THEY LEARNED ABOUT THEIR FLAWS? HOW? WHY? WHAT IS THE IMPACT OF THIS ON THE OTHER CHARACTERS? HOW DOES IT CHANGE THEM? WHERE IS THIS HAPPENING?

REMEMBER SHOW NOT TELL.

WHAT TRAITS ARE THE CHARACTERS INVOLVED SHOWING? WHAT EMOTION DO YOU WANT THE READER TO FEEL? EG. HOPEFUL?

WHAT COULD THE ANTAGONIST BE THINKING/DOING/FEELING? SHOW DON'T TELL.

THE COMPLETE PLAN FOR WRITING YOUR BOOK

30. THE PLAN? BY THE WAY, HOW'S THAT TICKING CLOCK DOING? WHAT COULD BE THE IMPACT ON ALL CHARACTERS? WHY?

WRITE DOWN THE POSSIBLE OUTCOMES AND WHY. ARE THE CHARACTERS DETERMINED? WHAT CONVERSATIONS ARE TAKING PLACE?

DOES ANYBODY DISAGREE WITH THE PLAN? WHY?

WHERE IS THIS ALL TAKING PLACE?

REMEMBER SETTING AND SENSES.

THE COMPLETE PLAN FOR WRITING YOUR BOOK

31. 'GATHERING THE TROOPS': WHO HELPS AND WHY? SHOW THE CHARACTER ADMITTING THEIR FLAWS IN AN EMOTIONAL SCENE AND ACTING COMPLETELY DIFFERENT FROM WHAT THEY DID IN ACT ONE. YOU COULD EVEN HAVE AN ALLY COMMENT HERE ON HOW THE MAIN CHARACTER HAS CHANGED.

REMEMBER SETTING AND SENSES.

WHAT KINDS OF THINGS WILL YOU WANT YOUR CHARACTERS TO SAY?

REMEMBER SHOW DON'T TELL.

WHO ARE THEY TALKING TO?

WHAT COULD THE ANTAGONIST BE THINKING/DOING/FEELING? SHOW DON'T TELL THIS.

THE COMPLETE PLAN FOR WRITING YOUR BOOK

32. EXECUTING THE PLAN: DOES THE CLOCK TICK DOWN TO ZERO? WHO IS INVOLVED? WHY? WHERE? WHEN? HOW? WHAT IS THE PACE OF THE SCENE? HOW CAN YOU SHOW THIS? WHAT CONVERSATIONS ARE TAKING PLACE? DOES ANYONE HAVE SECOND THOUGHTS? WHY?

WHAT COULD THE ANTAGONIST BE THINKING/FEELING/DOING? SHOW DON'T TELL THIS.

THE COMPLETE PLAN FOR WRITING YOUR BOOK

33. THE SUPRISE! THE "THING" ISN'T THERE! THE PLAN DIDN'T WORK (AT FIRST)!

PLOT TWIST TIME - MAKE IT MASSIVE!

WHAT COULD BE THE ABSOLUTE POSSIBLE WORST THING TO HAPPEN?

DOES SOMEBODY DIE? DOES SOMEBODY GET EXPOSED AS A DOUBLE-CROSSER? IF SO, WHY? HOW DOES THAT IMPACT ON THE STORY? HOW DOES EACH CHARACTER ACT AND WHY?

SHOW DON'T TELL THEIR TRAITS.

WHAT ARE THE CONVERSATIONS TAKING PLACE AND WHERE?

WHAT COULD THE ANTAGONIST BE THINKING/DOING/FEELING? SHOW DON'T TELL THIS.

THE COMPLETE PLAN FOR WRITING YOUR BOOK

34. WHAT HAPPENS NOW? IS THERE A DEBATE ABOUT THE PLAN? WHO IS INVOLVED? WHAT IS THE EMOTION IN THIS SCENE? HOW CAN YOU MAKE YOUR READER FEEL THIS EMOTION?

WHAT COULD THE ANTAGONIST BE THINKING/DOING/FEELING? SHOW DON'T TELL.

IF NOT ALREADY, IS THE CLOCK NEAR ZERO NOW? WHO IS INVOLVED IN THE 'LAST CHANCE' PLAN?

THE MAIN CHARACTER IS NOW A CHANGED PERSON. HOW DOES THIS LOOK? HOW HAVE THEY CHANGED? WHAT IS THE IMPACT OF THIS CHANGE FROM ACT ONE?

THE COMPLETE PLAN FOR WRITING YOUR BOOK

35. THE BIG BATTLE SCENE!

WHO IS INVOLVED?

WHAT CASUALTIES (PHYSICALLY AND EMOTIONALLY) ARE THERE?

WHO IS IMPACTED? HOW?

WHAT COULD THE ANTAGONIST BE THINKING/DOING/FEELING? SHOW DON'T TELL THIS.

THE COMPLETE PLAN FOR WRITING YOUR BOOK

36. SHOW THE MAIN CHARACTER IN THEIR NEW FORMAT.

WHAT IS THE IMPACT OF THIS?

REMEMBER, THIS SHOULD BE THE OPPOSITE TO HOW THEY WERE PORTRAYED IN ACT ONE.

THE COMPLETE PLAN FOR WRITING YOUR BOOK

37. WILL YOU LEAVE THE STORY ON A CLIFFHANGER? IF SO, WHAT WILL THAT BE?

WHAT WILL YOUR LAST LINE BE? MAKE IT INTRIGUING, ESPECIALLY IF THIS BOOK IS PART OF A SERIES YOU PLAN TO WRITE.

THE COMPLETE PLAN FOR WRITING YOUR BOOK

CONGRATULATIONS!

YOU HAVE COMPLETED YOUR FULL STORY PLAN!

NOW YOU CAN START WRITING YOUR BOOK!

USE THE SPACE BELOW TO MAKE ANY FINAL NOTES!

GOOD LUCK!

Well done!

We can't wait to hear about your book!

Contact us at:
HackneyandJones.com
and tell us how you're getting on.

Feedback

We'd love to hear what you thought of our **'How To Write A Novel From Scratch'** workbook.

Please scan the QR code below to leave your valued feedback.